My Cousin & Me
And Other Animals

Algonquin Wolf

Doe & Fawn

Barred Owl

Life size bronze statue of Huckleberry Finn (left) and Tom Sawyer (right) in Hannibal, Missouri, created by sculptor Frederick C. Hibbard.

Charles Darwin

Baby Raccoon

Fox Kit

Black Bear

Bull Moose

Every creature is better alive than dead, men and
moose and pine trees, and he who understands it aright
will rather preserve its life than destroy it.

Henry David Thoreau, *The Maine Woods*.

My Cousin & Me
And Other Animals

by

Gordon Harrison

Published by: *Prometheus Publications*
   Peterborough, Ontario
   Canada

Library and Archives Canada Cataloguing in Publication

Harrison, Gordon, 1936-, author
   My cousin & me : and other animals / Gordon Harrison.

Includes bibliographical references.
Issued in print and electronic formats.
ISBN 978-0-9879596-6-9 (pbk).--ISBN 978-0-9879596-7-6 (html)

   1. Harrison, Gordon, 1936- --Childhood and youth.
2. Human-animal relationships--Ontario. 3. Evolution
(Biology) 4. Ontario--Biography.
I. Title. II. Title: My cousin and me.

FC3075.1.H37A3 2016   971.3   C2015-907650-1
                                          C2015-907651-X

Cover design by the author
Picture of the author by Larry Keeley, D & L Photography

To my cousin and his mother and father
who made my boyhood summers so memorable.

CONTENTS

PREFACE

In the sun born over and over,
I ran my heedless ways

. . . .

Before the children green and golden
Follow him out of grace,
Dylan Thomas, "Fern Hill"

We left paradise when I was five and moved to the city to live with my mother's sister. I later learned, there were two reasons for this move: so that my parents could find work and I could attend school. My mother was sympathetic toward my desire to return to the farm, so every July 1 she took me back to paradise for the summer. I lived the rest of the year for those two months.

The farm was run by my aunt and uncle. And they had a son who was my companion in the exploration of the fields for deer, the forests for bears, fence posts for bird's nests, and ponds for the astounding gilled salamanders—we were Tom Sawyer and Huckleberry Finn. Anything that was alive we were interested in, anything beautiful we were fascinated by. I think this is the natural state of the young until society's norms steal it from them. This enchantment with the land and its creatures is still green in my memory; this joy is still felt in my heart.

My Cousin & Me: And Other Animals is a natural history memoir of two skinny boys chasing life in the hinterlands of Ontario unfettered and free, as we would never be again. Those years shaped all the ones that followed. Much of my adult life has been spent in photographing the creatures I had seen on the farm as a boy, and these pictures are liberally scattered throughout these pages. This book is an ode to the beauty of life created by evolution through natural selection.

Come, join my cousin and me as we walk out the door and turn toward the rising sun to seek the fields and forests for a thousand wonders. The future will not be like the past. Tomorrow will not be like today. Every day is different. You must catch the apple when it falls and sweet or sour bite it hard!

ACKNOWLEDGEMENTS

The genesis for this book has been a lifetime. I have always considered myself to be fortunate, especially so in having an excellent editor, Karen Taylor. She went through the entire book, word by word, offering innumerable improvements. I owe her a great debt. In writing this book, I have also been fortunate in having many friends who offered suggestions that have greatly improved the text. Bill Samuels diligently read the early drafts providing many suggestions and corrections. Jerry Larock was most helpful with the cover design. My partner, Evelyn, has been an important sounding board and a source of ideas and unending support. My daughter has listened to me rave about my photographs and has always been encouraging. Plus she pointed out many typos in the "finished" text. And Larry Keeley and Dawn Knudsen corrected numerous "blemishes" in the first printing. I am most grateful to everyone. An old proverb affirms, "Luck never gives; she only loans." But in the writing of this book, I've been Lady Luck's major beneficiary, and these gifts she can never take away.

Every reasonable effort has been made to contact holders of copyright for other images used here. The author will gladly receive information that will enable him to rectify any inadvertent errors or omissions in subsequent editions.

CHAPTER—1

A PLACE IN THE UNIVERSE

We shall not cease from exploration
And the end of all our exploring
Will be to arrive where we started
And know the place for the first time.
T. S. Eliot, "Little Gidding"

A MOTE—a mote in the eye of the universe. Near this mote is one of the largest structures in the cosmos, a gargantuan gathering of galactic superclusters into a single gravitationally bound assembly called the Laniakea (Hawaiian for *immeasurable heaven*). The mote, of course, knows nothing of this. It drifts.

The speck moves toward the Virgo Supercluster. Millions of years pass before it "enters" this cluster. After more eons, our mote moves toward a minor collection of galaxies called the Local or Home Group. This galaxy group comprises two magnificent island universes, the Andromeda and the Milky Way, each with its attendant minor galaxies. The mote coasts between these titans while they move toward each other. The larger Andromeda with its one trillion stars will eventually devour the smaller Milky Way. This latter island universe lies at the utmost edge of an insignificant tendril of the mighty Laniakea Assembly. The mote, of course, knows nothing of this. It drifts.

A Milky Way Look-Alike Galaxy: NGC 6744

Casually it floats toward the Milky Way and "close" to one of its smaller spiral arms, the Orion. After more eons, it approaches an ordinary star in this arm, the one we call the sun. Around this star is a collection of planets, asteroids, icy objects, comets, and debris. The mote drifts in the direction of the third planet from the sun.

It has been a long night's journey from the Laniakea Assembly to the Local Group to the Milky Way to the Orion Arm to a commonplace star and, ultimately, to the beautiful blue dot we call the Earth. As far as we know, this planet is the only place in the entire vastness of the universe that supports life. Everywhere else, you die instantly! Instantly!

Red Spot on the Blue Planet

The mote has arrived a billion years too late to participate in the greatest show on earth—the evolution of life. The forms are so wondrous, so varied, and so ingenious that the naive eye might conclude a grand designer did all this instead of evolution. Darwin would say all these wonders are the result of "descent with modification."

Unexpectedly, the mote knows something of evolution. For it was created in the core of a massive star and cast out on its long odyssey by a supernova explosion to wander the cosmos until it fell to earth on the Red Spot in the photograph of the "Blue Planet." As Carl Sagan says,

> The nitrogen in our DNA, the calcium in our teeth, the iron in our blood, the carbon in our apple pies were made in the interiors of collapsing stars. We are made of starstuff.

By chance, the mote landed on the 45th parallel, midway between the North Pole and the equator. Apparently, all of its incredible journeys were now at an end, but, as I said, it arrived late. Innumerable members of its family of elements had arrived in the previous five billion years: iron, oxygen, carbon.... These elements by processes science is now discovering combined and rose to consciousness and ultimately reflected on itself and the universe.

We are puny creatures! We are parasites devouring the third planet of an ordinary star, one of 300 billion, in a small arm of an out-of-the-way spiral galaxy, a minute part of the mighty Laniakea. Yet we are privileged to have a vision of creation built on evidence. We are splendid creatures! You and I are rolled out of stardust, baked in the furnace of creation. "What a piece of work is a man! How noble in reason! . . . in action how like an angel! in apprehension how like a god!" (*Hamlet*, Act II, Scene 2).

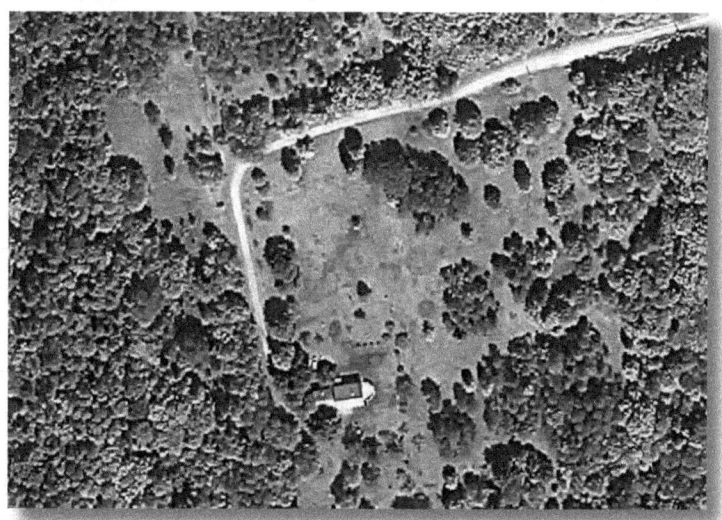

A Place in the Universe

This mote of carbon found itself in a jungle of grass, flowers, and weeds more abundant than Darwin's "entangled bank." The rains washed it into the soil and the following spring it was absorbed in the growth of a flower that some call a weed, others, the devil's paintbrush. These come in red and yellow swaths splashed across the wild fields of Ontario. All of this happened on my "lawn" in the red spot shown in the photograph. Look closely and you will see my home located at seven o'clock relative to the dot. The grass, flowers, and weeds grow luxuriantly here, directly over the septic system.

A white-tailed yearling deer, attracted by the rich pasture above the septic tiles, devoured the devil's paintbrush along with a mouthful of grass. And so the journey of the mote began again. Like Tennyson's "Ulysses," it cannot rest from travel. The following winter a pack of five wolves caught this yearling

Devil's Paintbrush

on a nearby frozen lake. After their feast, they ran into the wilderness of the evergreen forest. Now this mote of carbon was truly gone. Gone forever—lost in a vast and intricate landscape. But the mote wasn't the least inconvenienced by any of this. It was now running with the wolves.

The wolves run on through the evergreen forests in their eternal pursuit of the deer. And for their part, the deer lead the wolves on a deadly chase. Each hones the other to perfection by natural selection. It's not only the weak and the old who falter and fall; it's the inefficient—the ones who stray too far from the edge. To those who do the dance, whether deer or wolf, belongs the day and the future. It's not a good day to die. It never is. And so the wolves run on through the evergreen forests.

The Yearling

The Algonquin Wolf—*Canis lycaon*

In the last paragraph of *On the Origin of Species*, Charles Darwin—referring to evolution—writes one of the finest sentences in the English language:

> There is grandeur in this view of life, with its several powers, having been originally breathed by the Creator* into a few forms or into one; and that, whilst this planet has gone cycling on according to the fixed law of gravity, from so simple a beginning endless forms *most beautiful and most wonderful* [emphasis added] have been, and are being, evolved.

We will search this land for all its forms of life. We will turn over old barn boards and sheets of metal roofing to find snakes, ants, voles. We will look for birds' nests under eaves, in hollow fence posts, in bushes and trees. We will wade through creeks and search ponds for minnows, frogs, and salamanders. In the cool evening, we will listen for owls, wolves, and mysterious night noises and watch our porch lights for giant silk moths as big as your outstretched hand. We will watch the fields for bears,

---

* Interestingly, this phrase "by the Creator" was not in the first edition of November 1859. Due to popular pressure for the mention of god, it was inserted into the second edition of January 1860 and subsequently retained.

deer, and moose. We will revisit those secret places that, as boys, only we knew: places where snakes still shed their skin, gilled salamanders glide through shallow golden pools, and striped skinks dart away. And we will inspect rock piles for weasels and woodchucks. We will find those "forms most beautiful and most wonderful" that Darwin spoke of.

Come, let us walk together and see the world anew through the eyes of a child. We will explore this land, and, in the end, we will know this place for the first time.

CHAPTER—2

DOE, A DEER

My earliest memories are of animals: goldfinches, squirrels, minnows, frogs, and deer…. These are as clear to me as if they had appeared this morning rather than decades ago.

My family lived in a rambling old building called the Boyd House on Brady Lake not far from the Red Spot—a place in the universe. Mother was the cook for a large crew of loggers, sawyers, and drivers—the only woman among fifty men, and she loved it. Our large blue and white house was situated on a rise overlooking the lake, which seems much smaller now than in earlier years.

When you are a child, every day is sunny, even when it rains. So whether it rained and then the sun came out, or the sun was out and then it rained, I cannot recall. But I do know my mother called me to the window to see a doe and her fawn step out of the mist on the far shore of the glassy lake for a drink. From that moment until this, I have been as deeply "imprinted" as any of Konrad Lorenz's geese. The white-tailed deer is the quintessence of grace and beauty, a supreme example of the results of natural

Doe, a Deer, a Female Deer!

selection. Both animals, doe and fawn, hurriedly drank from the lake, turned and bounded away swallowed up by the eternal green forest. I never saw them again except in my mind's eye where they will never grow old or die.

At two years of age—and every year thereafter—females get pregnant and normally have one to three fawns in April or May. For their safety, mom visits her babies just a few times each day so they may nurse. Once the fawns can run (bound), mother and child are inseparable. By fall, their camouflage spots have vanished, and their coat darkens to blend with winter's hues and possibly absorb more sunlight.

I once cradled a fawn in my arms—it was a memorable experience, such a bundle of warmth, softness, and legs. Its complete and utter helplessness produced a protective instinct in me as if it were my own child. No, I didn't find this fawn on the forest floor but in a veterinarian's office on a table.

The occasion of it being there is a drama itself. Road-killed deer are a common occurrence in Ontario. A quick-thinking medical doctor who witnessed a pregnant doe dead or dying on the roadside performed an emergency caesarean section to rescue her twin fawns. The doctor rushed the fawns to my vet's clinic where one was DOA and the other still struggling for existence. Its adorability inspired everyone to do whatever he or she could that it might live. My vet even took the fawn home that evening,

Bambi in the Gooseberries

so she could care for it all through the night. It died from insufficiently developed lungs as I learned later. The material universe is not compassionate—it cares for neither you nor me, so we must care for each other and all living creatures.

A Fawn in the Grass

Fawns grow quickly! They have to. For if summer is here can winter be far behind? When winter comes, they must run *from* the wolves not *with* them, perhaps even from our carbon mote of the previous chapter. Does do not, however, abandon their fawns—the males stay with her for one year, the females for two.

Fawn in Fall with Flag Up Ready to Run

Madonna and Child   The Kiss

These seemingly mild and gentle animals are not defenseless. They have deadly two-pronged hooves and multi-pronged antlers. Bucks with a large rack will stand their ground against a pack of wolves and even gore a mountain lion before tossing it in the air like a plaything. Most animals will *stand and deliver* if the situation requires. There is a banality of heroism among all creatures great and small, including humans.

Consider the baby woodchucks pictured here:

Mother Woodchuck and Her Five Little Chips

While rambling through ancient fields near my grandfather's old barn, I noticed some movement in the grass. Investigating I discovered a very young woodchuck, popularly called a "chip." Since the nearest woodchuck den was about 300 yards (275 meters) distance, I surmised this little wanderer was leaving home permanently. Chips are weaned at six weeks and leave the birth burrow shortly afterward. Being herbivores, they are walking on their food.

My Grandfather's Barn Being Eaten by the Forest

The chip immediately sensed my presence and turned to face this terrifying challenge. Because the field was large and his den distant, he had little choice but to stand and deliver. To increase his size, he instinctively stood on his hind legs, scratching the air with his front claws all the while uttering an aggressive whistle. I marveled at his courage: he was Odysseus to my Polyphemus—man to cyclops. I wish he could talk or write that he might regale his children with tales of how one sunny afternoon a young silverback chip drove off a one-eyed giant. But nature's bravery is an everyday event, unheralded and quickly forgotten.

What is true for the lowly woodchuck is also true for the graceful deer. Every winter I put out "deer food"—a nutritional mixture of oats, cracked corn, and molasses. In three or more feet of snow, this food source is welcome and often needed, especially by the fawns and the older bucks and does. In the presence of such abundance, however, in an otherwise grindingly harsh environment, fights often erupt among deer. Analogously, humans often squabble over a rich parent's will. Jane Goodall observed similar behavior among chimpanzees in the presence of a large banana cache.

In winter, deer gather in groups on a much-reduced range called a deer yard. And it's these groups of a dozen or more that regularly came to my feeding center. When two or more does arrived with their fawns, the mothers frequently rose up on their hind legs to box with each other (*see* photograph). They do this to allow their fawns— their genes—to feed first. Clearly, selection pressure encourages aggression at bonanza sites. Those in the past, the distant past, who stood up and fought for their fawns to

You go for it Mom!

feed first were more likely to leave healthy progeny. Aggression increases the survival of the aggressor's genes. Remarkably, I have never observed anyone injured. However it could happen. Certainly, hooves hurt!

Herd at Feeding Area

Handsome and Dangerous

Antlers are grown and lost annually, unlike horns, which are grown once and last permanently. Bucks use their antlers to impress does and other bucks. Fights between bucks are uncommon; usually each sizes up the other and the less well endowed wisely retreats. Nonetheless, when two are evenly matched a fight will ensue and everything goes. The winner gets his choice of the ladies and his genes survive. Again, aggression increases the survival of genes—at least with deer.

An old cliché states that beauty is all in the eye of the beholder—that's partly true but not the whole truth. Beauty is something else, something objective we can measure. The one-antlered buck *is not as attractive* as his former self (pictured above the caption "Handsome and Dangerous") His lack of symmetry hints at a certain diminished virility, as does the cane of an old man. In some societies youth and

One-Antlered Buck

virility are synonymous with beauty. When your left side is identical to your right side (bilateral symmetry), people judge you to
be beautiful and healthy. Many mothers realize their infants prefer looking at symmetric rather than asymmetric patterns. Or
perhaps it's a form of imprinting; after all, the loving face that
babies first focus on has bilateral symmetry, providing a refer-
ence for security and survival.

In a broad sense, physical symmetry is related to health and
beauty—at least as applied to the bodies of mammals. Show me
an animal with a large asymmetry, and I'll show you a sick animal. Much of the cosmetic industry and the work of plastic sur-
geons attempt to retain or restore bilateral symmetry. On the
other hand, small exceptions can be intriguing—witness the
mole above the upper left lip of supermodel Cindy Crawford.

Ermine on Antlers

Bucks shed their antlers in
the New Year and clearly at
different times. Search for
them after the snow melts
and before the green growth
of spring, a time I call the
brown season. Their ivory-
like sheen contrasts with the
tanned forest floor, allowing
these gems to shine like a
beacon. Be aware that you're not the only one looking for sheds.
Mice, porcupines, and ermine[*] chew on the tines; even foxes,
wolves, and bears gnaw on the main beams, which are full of cal-
cium, phosphorus, and mineral salts. Once I discovered a colony
of yellow slugs on the tines of a massive antler.

White-tailed deer are wondrously evolved to deal with the
harshness of the north woods. And since this book celebrates the
results of evolution rather than its processes, let's see how.

The largest deer live furthest north; the smallest, in Florida
(the Key deer) and furthest south. Why should this be? The answer is simple, even elegant, and it works for other animals:
bears, birds, and beavers. As your size (volume) increases, your
skin (area) increases at a slower rate, and it's your total skin area

---

[*] In summer, ermine are brown short-tailed weasels.

The Afternoon of a Fawn

that cools you. That's why a large cup of coffee cools more slowly than a small cup—it has more coffee for less increase in paper. Mice, squirrels, snakes, and numerous other creatures also huddle for warmth; humans do as well. In a cold bed, we draw up our legs into a fetal position and pull our arms close to our bodies in an effort to reduce our surface area by becoming more spherical, so to speak. Dogs curl up like a ball; geese, swans, and other birds tuck their heads under their wings—examples are all around us. I once came upon an adorable fawn as I returned from a walk (*see* "The Afternoon of a Fawn"). Instinctively she had pulled her long legs under her body to reduce her surface area and so conserve heat.

Nonetheless, this fawn is resting directly on ice and snow—cold, penetrating, relentless snow. Deer in their darker, thicker winter coats, however, are impervious to such privations. Remarkably, under the area your thumbprint covers are at least a thousand individual deer hairs: outer, darker guard hairs and inner body-hugging, heat-retaining coats. These inner hairs are

Inner Deer Hair

hollow, so this fawn is wrapped in a million tiny thermos bottles. Snow falling on her back or face does not melt. Often in chance wanderings in the winter woods back of my grandfather's barn, I've happened upon a deer-bedding area—depressions in the snow on a small rise so they may be ever watchful for wolves, runners of these northern forests. These depressions provided little evidence any snow had melted from the heat of their bodies.

The Book of Psalms says, "I praise you because I am fearfully and wonderfully made." Great poetry, poor science! None of us is "made" as if by an intelligent creator. Rather we are "molded" by natural selection, and the products of this process are truly wonderful. And the writer of the Psalms was parochial in speaking only of human animals. We have seen, at least, one non-human animal that has been wonderfully molded by millions of years of descent with modification. In conditions in which we would quickly and miserably perish, they appear as if they had just stepped out of a grooming salon.

Our fawn resting on the snow will, with some good fortune, grow into the exquisite doe stepping out of the snowy wilderness—into another "Great Princess of the Forest."

The Great Princess of the Forest

The animal humans know and love best is the dog, *Canis lupus familiaris*. Dogs are domesticated wolves. Thousands of years ago, some wolves discovered that hanging around a campsite of hunter-gatherers was beneficial—these sites were excellent sources of free food. The hunters soon realized these semi-tame wolves could help in tracking deer and other game, and sound an alarm of unwanted nighttime intruders. Hunter and wolf became codependent and that bond continues to this moment. By careful breeding over just a few thousand years, we have created (molded) an unimaginable cornucopia of different dogs. Darwin called this process "artificial selection." Virtually every variety of plant and animal we eat is the product of our special selection—fruits are less seedy and sweeter; grains more plump and disease resistant; animals larger and less aggressive. By eating the fruit of the Tree of Knowledge, we have created the true Garden of Eden. The original banana was small, bitter, hard, fibrous, seedy, green, and inedible. Humans produced the modern banana. We imagine we are the lords of creation!

Over several decades, I have had three dogs, each with a distinct personality. Their loyalty and love for me was always puzzling—I felt I didn't deserve it. Remarkably, love between man and dog is documented by the first literature of Western civilization. Homer tells us that when Odysseus went to Troy he left behind his dog Argos known for his speed and strength. Upon his master's return after twenty years, the ancient dog recognized Odysseus, raised himself, wagged his tail, dropped his ears, and happily died. This is the world's first description of a *friendly* animal; it's accurate and it's a dog.

Ruffy: Friend, Companion, and Clown

To Ruffy
Who is forever chasing rabbits,
Birds, butterflies, and turtles
On the Happy Isles—home of all
Heroes and every brave being—
Nose down on the trail to happiness.

Dogs never complain. In his poem "Animals," Walt Whitman writes, "They do not sweat and whine about their condition." This is exactly so. My dog Ruffy was nearly blind in his last two years, but his condition never altered or diminished his cheery disposition. Often, if I had been absent, he would greet me by jumping up on long hind legs, throwing his huge front paws around my neck, and hugging me hard to show his hairy affection. And I loved it!

Anyone who is familiar with dogs can to some degree read their facial and bodily expressions: happy, sad, hurt, fearful, playful, hungry, angry, and so on. These expressions do not all look alike, as the bigot says of races other than his own.

If I say your dog shows human traits in his expressions, you are amused. If, however, I say you are showing the same traits as your dog, you may be annoyed. But is there any real difference? Darwin thought not. In 1872, the great naturalist wrote *The Expressions of Emotions in Man and Animals*. In it, he tries to show the universality of the expressions, of say pursing the lips in concentration or tightening the eye muscles in anger. He writes, "The young and the old of widely different races, both with man and animals, express the same state of mind by the same movements."

Now that we have established facial expressions in dogs, I'll do the same for white-tails. Consider the following eight deer with my caption of the feeling each was expressing. See if you agree.

Angry   Curious

Sleepy   Pissed

Weary   Alert

Uncertain   Relaxed

These pictures portray a wide range of expressions. I consider the last neutral or relaxed, and I'm uncertain what the fawn with its tongue out is expressing. Some readers may think I'm anthropomorphizing. To them I say look again and reconsider. There is something more here, another consciousness that is sometimes suffering and sometimes happy, and it shows.

The Buds of Spring

If the does, fawns, and bucks survive the extreme hardship of the dark season, they live another cycle. New antler buds appear on the foreheads of the bucks (*see* photo) to prepare them for the fall rut and the passage of their genes. Fawns are now yearlings and the males soon leave to make their own way in the wilderness. Does give birth, but female yearlings still tag along behind their mothers.

One fine spring day, when snow-free areas were appearing in my fields especially near trees, a yearling, having survived the winter and the wolves, rested under some sumacs within a few feet of the Red Spot. We knew each other from my winter feedings, so we weren't enemies. The yearling was more curious than concerned. As I knelt on one knee, he posed for his portrait. He rested for an hour, perhaps touching the earth for the first time in half a year. In a few days, he would feed, as the deer do every spring, on the fresh green grass above my septic system, and perhaps mature into a great prince of the forest.

Yearling under Sumac

Over the halcyon days of summer, I see few deer. They fade into the forest dark and deep. Their winter deer-yard area expands tenfold. The does are particularly secretive until their fawns can bound and bounce away to safety from bears, wolves, and eagles; the bucks are as elusive as unicorns. Despite the blackflies during the day and the blood-sucking mosquitoes of the night, they somehow survive to the fall. Their flag (tail) is too short to serve as a flyswatter—they just endure. Nonetheless, I *did* see my very first deer at the edge of a lake in summer. By fall, the hardships of winter, wolves, blackflies, and mosquitoes have been forgotten, and we have a time of ripening, as John Keats writes in his poem "To Autumn":

> *Season of mists and mellow fruitfulness!*
> *Close bosom-friend of the maturing sun;*
> *Conspiring with him how to load and bless*
> *With fruit the vines that round the thatch-eves run;*
> *To bend with apples the moss'd cottage-trees,*
> *And fill all fruit with ripeness to the core;*

Deer love apples. Several decades ago, I planted a small orchard of apple, pear, plum, and cherry trees. Deer, moose, bears, and occasionally wolves will travel great distances to eat this fruit. The adults among these animals, unfortunately, have their own special way to "prune" a fruit tree—it's not my method.

Fall Doe and Her Yearling

Apples?

Deer, moose, and bears have a special fondness for a certain kind of apple. Curiously, it may come from any variety of apple tree. What makes it special? Only that it is a windfall having lain on the ground long enough to ferment. These animals are not members of the Woman's Christian Temperance Union; they will eat such fruit until they are tipsy or drink till they are drunk. At this once-a-year party anything goes. Intoxicated moose have been found wedged in the crotch of apple trees, and deer stagger into traffic or pass out in the forest.

After the deer sober up, the season of terror arrives: the hunt. This period corresponds to the rut when deer are in prime condition and most vulnerable because of the inexorable drive to mate. The bucks fear no one—all their innate shyness is abandoned. Once during the rut, while I was in my orchard repairing the "pruning" an industrious bear had accomplished, a frenzied buck ran past me so close I could have touched him. For a split second, he glanced at me with frenzied eyes that rolled in their sockets and then he went on by. A feeling of relief rushed through me—he realized I was not a nubile doe worthy of mating with.

I have shot a thousand deer, but only with a camera. So every time I see a photograph I relive the whole experience, and, in some manner, the animal has an element of immortality.

Buck Eating Apples

White-tailed deer have taken a long, long time getting to today, and the road has been anything but straight. They never climbed an evolutionary ladder or ascended an evolutionary tree. The best metaphor we have is a bush or multiple bushes. No life form evolves in a predetermined fashion or direction: this is the false concept of orthogenesis (directed evolution). We're all on our way to nowhere not knowing whence or whither—as the *Rubáiyát* says, "*Into this Universe, and* Why *not knowing, Nor* Whence, *like Water willy-nilly flowing.*"

The very word "evolution" itself is misleading, implying a direction, specifically an upward direction. Many dictionaries give an incorrect definition for it—even as their primary meaning. Somewhere they will say we're evolving upward from the simple to the complex. Yet occasionally organisms, especially parasites, adapt by becoming less complex: the classic example is the tapeworm, just a head with a segmented stomach.

The correct definition of evolution implies no road map, and the preferred phrase is the one Darwin often used, "descent with modification." The notion that evolution has a direction—and worse an overriding purpose—is outmoded and false. All life forms have existed in a vast whirlwind of events over immense eras, forever adapting to the here and now or perishing. This is the condition of all organisms; it's also the human condition, and we must deal with it.

Opposed to the soft yearning for orthogenesis is the tough concept of contingent history: the idea that no particular path of evolution is inevitable. All outcomes are contingent on a multitude of quirks and accidents. In his splendid book *Wonderful Life*, Stephen Jay Gould fully develops the concept of contingent history with numerous detailed examples from the Burgess Shale. The book's title comes from Frank Capra's famous Christmas movie *It's a Wonderful Life*—Hollywood's unsurpassed example of contingency.

This Great Prince of the Forest (*see* photo) has endured innumerable contingencies and survived them all. May he continue to ride life's whirlwind. The picture was taken the last time I saw him. On a cold January morning, he took one last glance at me, stepped behind a white pine, and was gone.

The Great Prince of the Forest

CHAPTER—3

TURKEY SHOOT

And as I was green and carefree, famous among the barns
About the happy yard and singing as the farm was home,
In the sun that is young once only,
Time let me play and be
Golden in the mercy of his means. . .
Dylan Thomas, "Fern Hill"

C arl Sagan once remarked, "If you want to make an apple pie from scratch, you must first create the universe." What is true of apple pies is even truer of any living thing. A complete history of the tiniest organism would lead us back to the Big Bang. Fortunately we are not going to travel that far today.

Tom Turkey in Summer

In my memory, my cousin and I went out most late summer evenings to return the turkeys[*] to the safety of the barn. Since these birds were creatures of habit, we knew they had gone to the "spring field"—the grasshoppers were most plentiful there. Follow the food and you will find them! This outing was happy because by late summer the hordes of May-June blackflies and mosquitoes were gone. After supper we would race barefoot through the barnyard and turn down a cow path that led to this lower field.

Eventually we would find the turkeys pecking at grasshoppers and things we could not see buried in the entangled universe under our feet. Their crops would be so full, they each appeared to have swallowed a baseball; all this food mellowed their

---

[*] The photographs of turkeys in this chapter are all of *wild birds*.

normally skittish behavior. And with some difficulty—approaching that of herding cats—we somehow managed to get them into one of our many barns, safe from wolves, foxes, fishers, or whatever else.

On a few occasions—particularly when the grasshoppers were very plentiful—the turkeys would go to roost early, being unable to eat any more. And with these domesticated birds, roosting was always on the lower branches of a sugar maple tree. Now this presented a severe problem for my cousin and me!

Once roosted, these birds were difficult to dislodge. Let me try to describe our dilemma delicately. For those gentle readers unacquainted with bird anatomy let it be said that turkeys dispatch bodily liquids and solids through a single orifice. A combination not unlike rain and hail having the color of gray gravel glazed with an indescribable stench shoots out. And when frightened these percolating cauldrons released copious quantities of this devil's brew. For hatless and defenseless boys, scaling the tree was tantamount to taking Vimy Ridge unarmed. We wisely retreated.

Hen Turkeys up a Tree

At home we encountered no reprimand, no harsh words, not even disappointment from my uncle or aunt. Things, good and bad, were just accepted. In the morning, as I recall, the turkeys were always safe and contentedly consuming more grasshoppers and converting them into delicious drumsticks.

As I mentioned, before this time I had lived as the only child at a lumber mill where my father was the blacksmith and my mother, the cook. Mother was a tall woman with strong arms who had spent her younger years as a tomboy on the farm, milking cows, cleaning stables, and doing heavy fieldwork. When the owner of the mill asked her to be the camp cook for a crew of lumberjacks, she laughed and alleged she couldn't boil water without burning it. "Not to worry," replied the mill owner. "Flour and sugar are cheap." For two weeks my grandmother taught her daughter how to cook a few basics: bread, tea biscuits, butter tarts, pies, and so on. So off she went.

Mother was the essence of independence—there is a rumor she invented women's lib. It's no accident that Canadian women first won the vote in Manitoba and American women in Wyoming—independent farm ladies all. Every evening she coerced a gang of men to peel potatoes for the following day, to bring in wood, to wash dishes, and to do other chores—activities they would never have done at home. How did she do it?

The day everything changed was a Sunday early in May before the blackflies. There was to be a contest, a turkey shoot, a live hen* was to be awarded to the mill's top sharpshooter. A large bull's-eye was placed across Brady Lake on which the mill was located. All the men came from farms where hunting was a common practice. Fuelled by pride and testosterone, everyone fancied himself as great a hunter as Nimrod. More than 30 men used the rifle that day and while some missed the target entirely several hit within the middle ring—but none had penetrated the innermost circle. After everyone had had his two shots and there was no clear winner, Mother asked to fire a round. A few men guffawed, some smirked, and some knew full well that a woman couldn't shoot—a few knew better.

Time passed while several men argued about who was the winner, and by then the rifle barrel had cooled as Mother stepped into position. She raised her left elbow level with the gun stock,

---

* Hens are female turkeys, toms or gobblers male, jakes and jennies juveniles, and poults are babies.

quickly took aim, and slowly squeezed the trigger. The chap at the target on the far side of the lake—seeing a woman with a rifle—bolted into the woods. And he only emerged when the men shouted at him to see if mother's shot had possibly hit the target. Once assured that she was not going to shoot again, he approached the bull's-eye to see the result.

Hen Turkey

To this moment, I vividly recall him pointing to the center of the target and declaring her the winner. A few men guffawed again, some smirked, some knew full well that a woman could not shoot. Evidence to the contrary didn't matter. Two from this latter group got a boat and rowed to see for themselves. But it was so. Mother earned a lot of respect that day from the men, but she appeared unaware and unconcerned. She walked over, picked up this *tame turkey*, nonchalantly put it under her left arm, and strode back to the cookhouse as if this were the most natural event possible. Nevertheless, there would be no roast turkey that evening.

She fed the turkey oats from the horse barn and scraps from the kitchen. The bird would eat anything. At first it slept on a crossbeam in the woodshed, but before long it disappeared into the forest to roost. Our tame bird was going wild—but the back kitchen door still served as its take-out window.

Turkey Nest

Eventually it crept about most secretively. My father suspected it had a nest hidden somewhere, and it became my passion to find this nest. Mother, on the other hand, was looking for turkey eggs for breakfast, but father wanted to be certain she didn't find any. Turkey eggs are speckled with spots, at least twice the size of a chicken's, and three times as gamey—a delicacy reserved for practiced palates. Father would not eat them although he often sucked chicken eggs dry after poking a small breather hole in opposite ends.

I actively searched for the nest, trying to find it before Mother. Now a turkey's nest is a wondrous treasure: always on the ground, shaped like a circle the size of your encircling arms, and packed with paprika sprinkled *potential life*. My father found it under some bushes! The bird guides tell us the maximum number of eggs in a turkey's nest is 18, but I counted 22 that day. Still, as I said, a turkey's nest is a near miracle. For the child in each of us, this nest was equal to a box of baby kittens or a manger full of puppies.

Because of mother's diligence, it was inevitable that she would find the nest, but by the time she did the turkey had been incubating too long. The eggs were past eating and on their way to being poults. With this turn of events, Mother thought she might have a turkey farm. After the eggs hatched, I saw the hen and her brood a couple of times, but always at a distance. Once was during a thunderstorm when she covered them with her umbrella-like wings. A poult's down soaks quickly, so hypothermia is always close at hand. Feathers originally evolved for warmth and protection from rain—flying was a later gift.

It is an old wives' tale that a turkey, especially a poult, will look up at the sky during a rainstorm with its mouth open until it drowns. Although turkeys sometimes do tilt their heads skyward

Flock of Wild Turkeys

when it rains and remain in that posture for some time, scientists say the idea that turkeys drown that way is just a myth. As in so many places, Darwin's discoveries work here. The natural world would soon *select out* such self-destruction behavior, leaving behind much smarter closed-mouth turkeys.

All that summer we never saw the turkeys again until one day late in September, when the hen marched out of the forest with her parade of teenage progeny—jakes and jennies as we call them. I counted 17 in all. They were star-scattered dots on the hayfield near an old log barn. Predation is natural in the wild, hence the reason for large clutches. Somehow my parents and I marshalled them into the barn where Mother immediately fed them a pail of raw oats. Father—always looking for an easier way—said that since they had done so well on their own we should just let them be, be wild that is. Mother reluctantly agreed. Led by the indomitable hen, this flock of jakes and jennies swiftly vanished into the darkening forest, lair of fisher and fox. We never saw them again.

My aunt and uncle left the farm because of the physical hardships: no electricity, no running water, no central heating, and outhouses without toilet paper—just a ragged Eaton's catalogue. But we children were unmindful of this adversity.

Years later, my cousin sold the old house (with its five bedrooms and two staircases) for its logs. The happy rooms where we had run and played on rainy days were now valued only as a means of income—that the buyer never paid. Nothing remains: no colossal wreck, just weeds and wire bush. The barns were sold as well, and where horses and cows once held sway, fields of wild raspberry canes now hold court. And when the berries ripen, bears roam where the horses' stalls once stood. No one would know humans had lived here. Everyone had forgotten how green was our valley!

Nevertheless, if you know where to look, a solitary sign of human activity can be found. A hundred yards south of where the house once stood, a hand-dug well, framed with granite fieldstones, still exists. The wooden shed covering it is long gone, perhaps sold also, but, on the ground under dirt and moss, its poured concrete cap and collar yet survive. In one corner, the men inscribed the date of construction: September 1939—a momentous year!

These 100 acres of wilderness farm had been my uncle's and my grandfather's before him. Eventually I purchased the "back 40" from my uncle and built a cottage and ultimately a house near the Red Spot. Thomas Wolfe writes that you can't go home again, and that is truer than the author imagined. Nothing stays the same: not for an hour, not for a second. This constantly changing cascade of events was immortalized by the 5th century Greek philosopher Heraclitus in his adage "Man never bathes in the same stream twice." Or, as some later wit remarked, "Not even once." But a place may be what chaos theorists call a strange attractor—although events are never exactly the same, they are close: they cluster. I call this "clustering" home.

The Return of the Native

Once upon a time, there were true wild turkeys in Ontario, but by the early 1900s, they were extirpated (eaten). A *wild* turkey should not be confused with a *feral* bird which is just a domesticate that has escaped the barn. As I learned when a boy, these latter birds will not live through an Ontario winter. Four centuries of domestication have robbed them of needed survival traits—through artificial selection. Modern turkey farms raise birds with pure white feathers like the ones pardoned by the

Turkey Fighting Spur

American president every Thanksgiving. Breeders do prefer white feathers, so the plucked carcass has no color blotches— all the better to sell. They have also artificially selected to eliminate the two-inch (5 cm) fighting spurs (*see* photograph) on the back of the male turkey's leg— all the safer to control. Yet a tom turkey, wild or domesticated, is a formidable bird.

As my mother told me, a large tom attacked her repeatedly when she was a young girl on the farm, every time she crossed the barnyard. Incidentally, all our animals—pigs, cows, horses, chickens, ducks, geese, and turkeys—were "free range." Now my mother, as mentioned, was a free spirit. One day, catching the tom unaware, she delivered a swift kick to his backside. A few days later, the bird died and Mother felt guilty. Perhaps that's why she told me, but never her parents.

> *There once was an angry old tom*
> *Who was always bothering my mom*
> *When caught unaware*
> *She kicked his large derriere,*
> *And that was the end of old tom!*

Our old-fashioned farm turkeys and true wild turkeys are difficult to distinguish. It is true that the wild variety generally weighs less, which allows them to fly a few hundred yards or meters and glide even further. The secret for telling them apart is on the tips of their tail feathers. Domesticated turkeys retain the white tail tip of the original Mexican subspecies from which they were derived. We use that marking to distinguish wandering barnyard birds from true wild turkeys, which have chestnut-brown tail feather tips like the large jake pictured below.

A Jake has Tail Feathers of Different Lengths.

In 1984, the Ministry of Natural Resources (MNR) embarked on an ambitious program to reintroduce wild turkeys into Ontario.

The MNR traded otters, fishers, and moose to various US states for wild turkeys, which the ministry released throughout the southern and central regions of the province. This reintroduction went spectacularly well: the wild turkeys lived, they thrived, they bred, and they greatly expanded their range.

Rumors of this success were everywhere: in the newspapers, on radio, and on TV. Then, one day in the middle of April when the woods were still clogged with snow and only a few brown patches appeared in my fields, I saw them. Like Alexander's Ragtime Band, a group of hen turkeys marched up through my orchard—perhaps for the first time in 150 years . . . perhaps for the first time ever. I wouldn't have been more impressed had they been playing "When the Saints Go Marching In." Male turkeys heard the hens' parade and quickly followed.

Many of the wild turkeys in my area go to the nearest town some 8 miles (13 km) for the winter months. Bird feeders, scraps, and handouts trump snow, wilderness, and predators. One year, however, two large toms overwintered with me. The food here was also free since they ate with the deer, blue jays, squirrels, and other creatures. Both deer and turkeys were wary of each other but curious as well.

Tom Turkey in Winter

Every afternoon, just before sunset, these two toms displayed some bizarre behavior. Taking turns, they stood outside my kitchen window, looking from side to side but facing south, in what appeared to be an agitated state. Suddenly, they pumped their wings mightily and flew with determination to the top of the tallest white pine tree in sight. Domesticated turkeys who are less streamlined and heavier could never achieve such heights, although some could fly to the top of our barn. After the first tom was safely sitting high in the tree, the second bird, encouraged by his friend, repeated the same act. At this exposed altitude, they frequently endured night temperatures of −30° F (−34° C) with driving gale force winds. Why would they suffer such apparently unnecessary hardship? At that height, they were likely to avoid their main predator, the fisher. Their only concession to the crushing cold was to face into the wind to prevent the ruffling of their feathers. *See* photographs below.

Two Tom Turkeys up a White Pine

In North America, turkeys have an undeserved reputation for being "mentally challenged" and are generally maligned. It wasn't always so. I suspect that, because of this reputation, the citizens of Turkey call them the American bird. Benjamin Franklin, we know, admired these birds so much that he recommended they be the national symbol of the USA rather than the bald eagle. At Thanksgiving, someone always trots out this story to entertain us. But perhaps Franklin was right. Naturalist and painter John James Audubon thought so highly of them that the gobbler (cock) was depicted on the first color plate of the first volume in his monumental *The Birds of America*; the hen was the sixth plate of 435. (*See* photographs below.) Audubon had a "wild" turkey as a pet that spent its nights on the roof of the naturalist's home. For its safety, Audubon's wife tied a scarf around the bird's neck, but it was shot nonetheless.

Plate VI: Hen and Poults

John James Audubon's
The Birds of America

Plate I: Turkey Cock

From comparing chromosomes, research scientists know turkeys are more closely related to dinosaurs than to other birds. And birds are the closest animals we have to these ancient reptiles. Even as turkeys, they have been around for ten million years—incredibly longer than humans. Their visual acuity and exceptional hearing are both beyond those of humans, and they sprint faster than an Olympic athlete. Evolution has equipped them with a range of abilities few can equal. They are our modern velociraptors.[*]

One afternoon while broadcasting raw oats on my lawn, near the Red Spot, I was spied by half a dozen toms from a distance of 300 yards (275 meters). Without hesitation, they bolted in my direction. Fortunately I wasn't being attacked by modern velociraptors but merely mobbed by semi-tame turkeys. Within seconds, the largest bird was at my side as I continued tossing out oats for them; the food even landed on their backs. Little wonder Audubon had one as a pet. He made an excellent choice.

---

[*] Velociraptors had a prominent role in the famous movie *Jurassic Park*. The producers, however, doubled their size and omitted their feathers probably to discourage any comparisons to turkeys, which were mocked early in the movie.

Head of a Modern Dinosaur

Just before sunrise on any spring morning, you can step out my door and you will hear ten thousand frogs completing their nightly oratorios. From nearby "Walden Pond" the booming call of the bittern echoes from the cattails, saying this land is his land. The whip-poor-wills have already put away their mysterious hypnotic melody and gone to roost. The night shift is over; the day shift is in progress. And just as our star peaks over the eastern horizon to reveal many fog-covered lakes, the triumphant call of the wild turkey cock erupts. All up and down my green valley his gobble, gobble, gobble resonates, and it sings of life. Its voice had been absent for half a century—since the days of two skinny boys chasing domesticated turkeys back to the barn in the darkening hinterland of Ontario.

Nothing I cared, in the lamb white days, that time would take me
Up to the swallow thronged loft by the shadow of my hand,
In the moon that is always rising,
Nor that riding to sleep
I should hear him fly with the high fields
Dylan Thomas, "Fern Hill"

CHAPTER—4

A SNAKE IN THE GRASS

A snake lurks in the grass.
Virgil, *Eclogues* 1.93

When the earth was young and the summers green and carefree, my cousin and I would roam the fields in search of whatever we might find. We had no prescribed duties, except perhaps bringing the cows or the turkeys to the barn at dusk; we were rather the keepers of berry patches and bluebird nests. Since we weren't in search of rare animals like moose, wolves, or bears, we were never disappointed. Hollow fence posts had to be inspected for birds' nests, ponds for tadpoles, swamps for turtles, pools for gilled salamanders, and special hidden places we alone knew for snakes and the occasional blue skink.

We were unfettered in our natural interests. As far as we knew, the adults in our lives had little interest or knowledge of the world outside. Rarely did they speak about it—hardly a bird's name or a flower's location. Infrequently, an aunt would express some fear or other, especially about poisonous snakes—we never found one—or skinks that might run up inside your pant leg to do great damage or the ever-vicious wolves.

On one occasion, a not too likeable aunt with an ugly goiter asked my cousin and me to capture a snake long enough to wrap around her neck twice, and then to release it before sundown. Local "wisdom" affirmed this would cause the goiter to shrivel up and disappear. Since she *feared* snakes, and we didn't particularly care for her, we quickly granted her wish. The common garter[*] snake with its beautiful multicolored stripes was the first choice. They are large and easy to find, and, as an additional benefit, they exude a foul-smelling musk from their anus perfect for our aunt's "treatment." As bad boys, we knew this stench would linger on her neck for a few days. To us the quest was fun, for our aunt it was a desperate attempt at a cure. Trusting adult wisdom, we fully

---

[*] Named for men's old-fashioned garters, the kind my father wore.

expected the wretched disfigurement to vanish, but that never happened. So I learned grown-ups were not always wise.

In the two years following the snake debacle, my aunt tried various faith healers and herbalists, but by the time she sought *proper* medical treatment, the growth had turned cancerous and spread. She died at forty-seven. That night, my extended family was at the hospital seated in a ring filling the entire waiting room—this was my first experience of death. My uncle was so devastated by his wife's passing that he never recovered. Her son, an older cousin, also died young. So much tragedy flowed from this superstition about the healing power of snakes. In human history, snakes have been the talisman of both life and death: from the rod of Asclepius to the viper's bite of Cleopatra's breast, these legends litter our lives.

Detail of a Garter Snake in the Wood Pile

Unfortunately, my cousin was ensnared by a belief in hucksterism and herbalism as well. As we grew up our roads diverged, his to the occult, mine to the more rational, although we were and always will be friends.

What makes a snake a snake? Well Genesis 3:14 (NIV) has this answer:

> So the Lord God said to the serpent, "Because you have done this,
> "Cursed are you above all livestock and all wild animals! You will
> crawl on your belly and you will eat dust all the days of your life.

In the halls of my high school was a very large skin of a snake with vestigial legs. Although no teacher explained this phenomenon, experts tell us primitive snakes, such as pythons and boa constrictors, do have legs beneath their skins and tiny, half-inch claws that protrude out of these nubs near the anus. No other snakes have legs. On every continent except Antarctica, however, there are *legless* lizards. So snakes may have legs and lizards may not. Clearly, the writer(s) of Genesis had no knowledge of either.

So if leglessness is not the defining characteristic, I repeat the question, "What makes a snake a snake?" Their most obvious feature is the absence of eyelids and eardrums—*see* the detailed photograph of the garter snake in the wood pile. So we can be certain that, in the Garden of Eden, the serpent never spoke, never heard, and never winked at Eve, naked as she was.

Puff Adder aka Eastern Hognose Snake

Most people remember their first encounter with a snake—I do. It's possibly my earliest memory. I was approaching the screen door to the cookhouse at the lumber mill and saw a chunky snake curled up, head and throat flattened and hissing terribly with a long forked tongue. I burst open the door to the kitchen and cried "mom." She responded like a rescue worker, battered the snake to death, and tossed it into the surrounding forest. Everyone at the mill called these colorful creatures puff adders, but I later learned they are also called hognose snakes because of their upturned snouts. They may be the most interesting reptile in North America. And they are completely *harmless*.

As a child, I witnessed only the first act in the puff adder's two-act defense drama. All the hissing, tongue flicking, and flattening of the neck was very like a cobra. On that distant summer day, none of us saw its ingenious second act. If the initial scene fails to deter a predator or assailant, the snake *pretends to faint*. Most predators will not eat dead prey: road kill and carrion require specialized stomach acids if those who eat either are to avoid infection—the kind of acids vultures have. To enhance the fainting act the snake will roll onto its back, open its mouth, hang its tongue to one side, vomit, and defecate some foul-smelling fluid—an act with special effects. So playing dead and doing it very well, as the hognose snake does, has distinct evolutionary advantages. Possums also know this trick. All predators notice movement first; stand still and you disappear into the landscape.

Playing Dead

As I alluded to earlier, there are *no poisonous snakes* in my area. Without such certain knowledge, we are wise to treat all snakes with respect—what's called a *false positive*. There is no penalty for considering every snake poisonous, as my mother did with the puff adder. In most places on earth, assuming snakes are poisonous is a true positive. Worldwide estimates by the Global Snake Bite Initiative suggest that at least 100,000 people die from snakebites every year, and another 250,000 are disabled. However many false positives you may have, avoidance of snakes is universal, and this evasion increases your life expectancy. Indiana Jones says it best in *Raiders of the Lost Ark*, "Snakes. Why'd it have to be snakes?"

In a similar vein, my grandmother would not eat mushrooms from the forest. She called them all "toadstools." I can still hear her proclaiming, "They're poisonous!" And certainly we have many deadly varieties on the farm, so this was a *true positive*. Without evidence-based knowledge to the contrary, she took a wise course of action. Really potent hallucinogenic mushrooms grow near the Red Spot.

If you always obey authority figures in your world—parents, priests, politicians, teachers—you will probably live longer and leave more children with obedient genes like your own. For this reason, systems of authority such as religion have survived for tens of thousands of years in every culture. Yet there is danger here, a danger different from that posed by venomous snakes and poisonous mushrooms. The "poison" of which I write is particularly deadly for the young of all species whether bear, beaver, or boy.

Someday every creature must grow up, and, if all you know is to follow authority and imitate your parents, how do you judge novel situations, events, or foods? (Here I am writing about humans.) If a plague hits your region, you pray; the plague persists and millions die. An unknown disease hits your crops so again, you pray; thousands more starve to death. So obeying authority does not always lead to survival. Among all creatures, humans adjust to the world as it is by using knowledge, knowledge derived by science, whether this knowledge is the making of fire with sticks or curing the Ebola virus with a vaccine. And science recognizes no authority but reality. These characteristics—the drive to know, to rebel, and be curious—define our species more than any other.

The theme of obedience versus disobedience is, in a broad sense, the essence of human culture and, to lesser degree, of non-human behavior. Allusions to it are scattered all through Western literature from Genesis to *Paradise Lost*.

Adam and Eve made the right choice by eating the fruit from the tree of knowledge. We are an ever-curious species with unlimited potential for intellectual growth and adventure, and we will pull the bear's tail. Our liberation came from listening to the snake. We will eat of the tree of knowledge—nothing will stop us. Had Adam and Eve not eaten from the tree, it always would have been midnight in the Garden of Eden.

Snakes play a disproportionate role in our lives, literature, and lore. A favorite of mine, because of its remarkable patterns, is the milk snake (*see* photograph). As boys my cousin and I often saw them lying on the hay in the barn bathed by light streaming through the gaps in the boards with a million specks of dust dancing in the sunbeams. Local wisdom claimed they sucked the udders of the cows during the night. Even as boys we suspected they were just waiting for mice, and when they caught one they would coil around it crushing out its life, for they are constrictors.

Milk Snake

As I mentioned previously, my cousin and I were bad boys, very bad boys. Most snakes we found we killed, and often we skinned them, drying their hides in the sun. After, we would store these prized objects in the bottom dresser drawer in our upstairs bedroom of the farmhouse. This hiding place may not have been entirely wise. Just once, and that was often enough, my aunt opened the drawer for some reason and her piercing cries still fill my ears. So incredibly loud were her shrieks that, as I recall, the sow in the barn aborted her litter, all the hens laid eggs, and the dog was found whimpering by the woodshed door. As boys, we had acquired the adult loathing for all things serpentine, and this murderous hunt was the result. Fortunately, we grew out of it.

In recent years, a few sheets of corrugated metal roofing have blown off the roof of the old barn onto the surrounding fields. At the right time in the morning, since snakes are cold-blooded, they will congregate under these sheets to warm themselves. Once I counted 16, from four different species, and the milk snake was often one of them, which seemed unusual as smaller snakes are part of its diet. Each sheet was my own private serpentarium.

One of the most beautiful creatures you will ever find is the one my cousin and I nicknamed the emerald snake, boringly called the smooth green snake (shown in photo). By the dead grass in the photograph, you can correctly infer it was under one of my metal sheets. Because their camouflage is so perfect when they are in the grass, they are seldom seen. And as boys, we counted them a rare find and never killed one.

Emerald Snake aka Smooth Green Snake

One crisp, clear morning late in October, I went out in search of fruit trees to transplant, and I knew where to find them. All the fall leaves of red and yellow now carpeted the forest floor and only the tamarack needles glowed with a golden hue. The land was quiet as if waiting for the first frost or snow. Once or twice a bird, perhaps a late migrant, called in its autumnal voice and then fell silent again. The land appeared asleep, but was just resting. No human being lived near me, not even close.

My grandfather had three plum trees whose fruit turned purple, red, and orange when ripe and tasted delicious. All around these ancient trees were their progeny germinated no doubt from castoff plum stones left by bears and boys. The closest any living thing gets to immortality is leaving offspring, and these trees had triumphed.

I dug up two, each about 6 feet (183 cm) tall that I intended to replant near the Red Spot at my home. While shoveling around the second tree, I uncovered a small treasure, a hibernating smooth green snake—I marveled that it was not below the frost line. So as not to warm it with my hands, I gently replaced it in the hole and covered it with soil to its former depth. Some snakes group together and pass the winter in what's called a hibernaculum. This little guy was a hermit, alone in the stone-cold ground. But life persists, and life will find a way. This was a simple event, but I realized I was no longer a boyish killer of snakes. My transplanted trees flourished in the following years; I hope that little snake did as well.

I've mentioned three of the four different snakes often found in my metal serpentariums: garter, milk, and emerald. The fourth is Ontario's smallest, an elfin creature the size of a pencil. It may dress in a brown, gray, or black snakeskin coat, but its belly is always red (*see* "Red-Bellied Snake"). As boys, my cousin and I were dutifully informed that these were deadly poisonous. These reptiles were incorrectly called copper snakes because of their crimson bellies. The adults had rhythms and riddles for instruction and entertainment:

> *Kill the first snake in the spring*
> *And good luck to you it will bring*
> *Miss the snake and let it live*
> *Will be the worst thing you ever did.*

Red-Bellied Snake

Yet these are harmless and delightful little snakes. In the past, all humans treated the wilderness and its wildlife as the enemy to be subdued, killed, eaten, or skinned. It has been a long night's journey into light, and we're not there yet.

I was about four years old when I had my encounter with the puff adder that my mother quickly dispatched. All that summer at the lumber mill, I never met another snake. After those peaceful days, we spent the winter at the mill. Now the men required even larger meals than in the summer months because they were sawing and chopping huge trees *by hand* and skidding them out of the forest with horses onto the lake. The only piece of power equipment was the giant steam engine that ran the large circular saws in the mill itself. For half a year, November to May, everyone was snowed in.

I loved the trips to town, 12 miles (20 km) away, with me in the back seat of my dad's car. The first trip in the spring was especially exciting; I was like a horse free from a winter's confinement in the barn. The roads were just mud, rock, and dirt, with a few corduroy sections, yet none of these inhibited my dad's headlong rush to town. I excitedly waited for the junction,* which I mistakenly thought was a large open water bog before the actual crossing itself. There was no bridge at the bog, just a makeshift causeway

---

* The crossing of the Peterson and the Bobcaygeon roads.

of logs and slab wood resting on a dark, spongy "floor." As the road sank, the men from the mill would pile on new wood. When we approached it that first spring, even this wood was missing. All I could see from the back seat was large expanse of black water as flat as glass. Nonetheless, my father started to drive over it! Even at my tender age, I knew you couldn't walk, least of all drive, on water. My mother shouted some unfamiliar words convincing me she held a similar opinion, but father continued. What neither of us knew or could see was the still existing "bridge" hidden two hand widths below the water's black surface. He drove across.

The summer trips to town, if less exciting, were more interesting. The now visible "bridge" was alive with basking turtles and huge water snakes (*see* photograph). I spent the whole trip in anticipation of seeing these chunky leviathans and was rarely disappointed. The vibrations generated by the car's approach would induce the serpents to slither off the boards into the water and quickly disappear in the labyrinthine crevices of the "bridge." It seemed to me that my dad aimed the car's wheels perilously close to the elusive snakes—Mother was oblivious to all this.

I came to realize the purpose of my father's rushing was the town's beer parlor and his need to forget the enduring hardships of the forest and the land. On our way back to the mill in the gathering darkness, his drinking made the journey across the bog even more hazardous. But I dreamed only of birds, animals, and snakes.

Northern Water Snake

When Men Were Machines

I soon came to realize this *junction* was the crossing of two roads, but understanding the predicament of my father came much later. As my childhood merged into boyhood, youth, middle age, and now beyond even that, I have long since forgiven his binge drinking. The physical labor of the forest and the mill was brutal, dangerous, and ultimately dehumanizing.

The town's residents who assuredly had fathers, uncles, or grandfathers from those days shared my late enlightenment. To commemorate these logging pioneers a heroic statue was erected by the town's river. The perfect inscription reads "When Men Were Machines." Theirs was a heroism they never knew and probably never felt. Mother, who also worked unbelievably hard, was unaffected—she seemed born to the plough. My parents shielded me from this dark pain, so I dream now as I dreamed then of deer, birds, and snakes.

CHAPTER—5

BEARS, OH MY!

A bear's days are warmed by the same sun,
his dwellings are overdomed by the same blue sky,
and his life turns and ebbs with heart-pulsings
like ours and was poured from the same First Fountain.
John Muir, naturalist, "On Finding a Dead Yosemite Bear," October 1871.

S ince we were young and carefree in the forest and the fields, we marched to no drummer but our own. Every day was endless and the summer an eternity. Although my cousin and I were not in search of moose, wolves, or bears, we did on rare occasions find one. Such a discovery would not be mentioned to the adults of our world for fear they'd restrict our ramblings to the house and the barns. On this fine day, we had gone into the forest behind the hand-dug well with the 1939 marker, and we turned east toward the rising sun. Perhaps we looked for berries—we were always looking for berries.

Not long after starting, my cousin picked up a rotten smell, a whiff of decay—his nose was always keener than mine. Being boys and adventurous, we followed our noses like hunting dogs

Black Bear on Stone Wall

on the scent of a deer. This foul stench increased rapidly, and soon we saw it lying on the forest floor dappled by the sun. Here was the rotting carcass of a once great bruin of the north woods. Yet death was alive with a million maggots. We were mesmerized! We must have watched this roiling carcass for 20 minutes with our T-shirts pulled up over our noses.

At the same moment we both decided to do it! We would take some part of the bear home as a souvenir. What part? Most of the enormous skull was bare and therefore free of maggots, so we determined to each take an eye tooth. These were large and securely anchored into the jaw, so we used a small granite rock to hammer the teeth free (*see* photograph of the bear skull). After this, I polished the trophy tooth on my pants and slipped it into a pocket; my cousin did the same.

Why did we do this? I'm not certain. Perhaps we felt the same urge as less complex people of the past who had entire necklaces of wild animal teeth—trophies of the hunt. I had this memento of a great animal's death for years, but like my youth I have misplaced it. Perhaps it's still here somewhere; maybe I should look around.

Skull of a Black Bear

Years later I reflected on *how*—not *why*—this bear died in that place at that time. Now without evidence you are left with an educated conjecture or a crude superstition; I wanted none of the latter. In the wild, black bears can live upward to 30 years, but rarely do. Most are shot by hunters or killed by cars long before they reach that age.

One night when I was in the back seat of the family car, which my father was driving back to the lumber mill, he *purposefully* hit a bear while we were driving uphill. Mother shouted out the same unfamiliar words I heard previously at the bog crossing. The car, however, was too light to inflict real damage, but it did anger the bear so much that he ran through a fence pulling up two posts. It seems unlikely, on the other hand, our trophy bear was shot because it wasn't hunting season, and we had heard no tales of a local Nimrod slaughtering bears. I conjecture this bear died of old age. He was on his way to pick blueberries, like my cousin and me, and, at this place and at that time, he had lain down to rest never to rise again. Every creature has a last step, a final beat, in a train of billions—all good things end.

I have referred to this bear as "he" because of his great size: males are generally twice as large as females, both as cubs and adults. And they need to be large to defend their territories from competing boars (male bears). Also the older the bear the bigger. The large boar in the photograph with his paws neatly folded seems to be implying, "Yes, I have been a very good boy." I consider this animal to be approximately the same size as the trophy bear we discovered so long ago on that fine day.

Mister Big

My cousin no longer walks these fields and forests with me, but not because he wouldn't want to. In those sunny summer days of meandering, we never once saw a live bear, although many may have seen us. All authoritative texts refer to *Ursus americanus*, the black bear, as "a shy woodland creature." Other than the trophy bear, I have never encountered another carcass. Nevertheless I now see live bears from April to November, sometimes several different ones each day. The bruins I meet have diverse personalities, yet they don't visit me because we are friends. Completing their billion steps, they wander freely near my home because we are not enemies. Bears are *normally* solitary.

Here is a gallery of extraordinary bears I have known:

At my latitude, April 10 is the average date for a bear to emerge from hibernation. On April 23, I noticed a bear walking toward the back of my empty pickup truck in which I often transport food. I assumed this bear was looking for a snack.

Then he does something incredible! Here is an animal who knows nothing about trucks, and might never have seen one previously. Yet he effortlessly twists the handle clockwise on the cap of my truck, flips the door into the up position, and hops in the back. Instinctively, I grab my camera and bolt from the door of the house. Knocking on the truck's cap, I calmly say, "Come on out, big fella." He responds to my request by hurling my plastic recycling box from the truck as an Olympic athlete casts a

Barney the Black Bear

javelin—and almost as far. At that moment, I had a revelation that what I was doing was dangerous, perhaps extremely dangerous. But before I could have a second thought, the bear is out of the truck facing me just a *body* length away. Again acting instinctively, if not wisely, I take his picture. The great portrait artist Yousuf Karsh couldn't have been happier with the result (*see* "Barney the Black Bear").

As you can infer from his portrait, this bear was not angry or shy but rather curious—let's call him Barney. I suspect he was about a five- or six-year-old male—almost every bear without cubs in the spring is male. I talked to him in quiet, soothing tones telling him not to go in the back of my truck again. Perhaps he should go look for a lady companion, I softly whispered. He did neither. He ambled a few feet away and sat on my grandfather's stone fence in the most relaxed fashion possible. Fear left my body and I continued to take his photograph for some minutes before he lumbered off.

Barney Bear Relaxing

I saw him often that summer, and he always had a relaxed easy-going manner. We were not enemies; we were not friends. But we were acquaintances.

Later that summer, one of my regular visitors was the nubile young princess pictured above the caption "Pretty Woman." Rarely do you see a wild animal this well coiffured; all she needed was a bow in her hair, I thought. She was perhaps 3.5 years old and not yet gravid, a perfect mate for my acquaintance Barney. Females (sows) are impregnated every two years throughout their mature lives and deliver one to three cubs in the winter.

Pretty Woman

Like humans, bears are promiscuous. Unlike humans, some of whom are ready for sex 365 days and 24/7, bears mate in July. If "Pretty Woman" didn't breed with Barney, then one of the local louts had that pleasure. A sow ready to mate attracts a retinue of admirers. I once had a young female lope up my driveway; over the next three hours, eight males followed her.

Local Lout   Another Local Lout

Large Lout

Extra Large Lout

Fermenting Apples

Bears are the stuff of legends, dreams, and childhood. They are teddy bears or vicious killers, saints or villains—maybe they are neither. They can, however, be the stuff of humor. Consider the four photographs of the bear that appears to be inebriated. Windfall apples had been fermenting for a time under some of my large apple trees, and this ruffian had eaten as many as his stomach would allow. He seems to know he has been imbibing and regrets it—a bear hangover.

Oh boy, what a hangover!   My tummy hurts!

Look at these love handles!   Oh, what an itch!

Mother and Cub on June 5

Whether Pretty Woman or the other sows breed with Barney or a local lout, any cubs will be born around Groundhog Day. At that time of year near my home, the temperatures can plummet to as low as –40°. Worse yet, each helpless cub weighs about 10 ounces and lives in a hole in the ground with a hibernating mother. Death seems imminent! Still, such is evolution, bears are not put in a situation they cannot survive. "Whatever does not kill me makes me stronger," writes Nietzsche.

Yet how do they survive? How is it possible? First, hibernation for bears is not a vegetative state but more of a torpor inducing only a slight drop in body temperature. One glance inside a bear's den and the wide unblinking stare of the sow will convince you of this fact—and of the wisdom of a very hurried retreat.

Mother and Cubs on July 18

The den is small so the mother's body can heat it, and the cubs snuggle for life itself. Although the sow neither urinates nor defecates all winter, she will lactate rich milk, so the cubs can grow quickly. The mother licks her cubs to stimulate defecation and then eats their feces to keep the den clean—this is premium day care. To see how rapidly cubs grow, compare their size in the two pictures taken just five weeks apart.

Peek

Like human children, bear cubs have much to learn. Unlike human children, bear cubs obey instantly. Lesson number one—taught before they leave the safety of the den site—climb a tree when danger is present. At my back door is an enormous white pine tree, and the cub pictured peeking out from behind it was watching me. The cub's sibling was even higher up this tree. Apparently, their mother saw me (the danger) through the window and sent her cubs skyward—a wise false positive. For extra, and may I say unnecessary, insurance, she stood guard at the tree's base. After some minutes, the sow, with a few meaningful grunts, summoned her cubs to scramble down, and then they vanished into the engulfing forest. Lesson taught, learned, and used!

Cubs also spend much of their day playing and some of this fun involves climbing trees. The sturdy youngster taking a "time out" has exhausted himself playing and naps in a tree—note his eyes are shut. Playing and learning are inextricably bound together and prepare all mammals for life's contingencies. *I play therefore I am!* And play is not unique to mammals. I have seen hawks, blue jays, and ravens frolic; the latter will even create patterns in the snow with their wings.

Time Out

Madonna and Child

Unless you have children, you cannot fully know the remarkable bond between parent and child—both human and nonhuman (*see* photographs of mothers with their cubs). Cubs stay with their mother for approximately 17 months; all the while she is protective and affectionate. During the first summer, they nurse every day cradled between mother's legs as she licks their bodies. And, in the fall, they will take the long sleep together, snuggling for warmth, with mother's body blocking the den entrance. But next summer everything changes!

The following June, the sow becomes very intolerant of her cubs and attempts to drive them away—or so the textbooks say. Yet this is not what I have observed from my home. Rather the parting is more like the one that occurred between the "Little Lady" and her mother. The mother commanded her obedient cub (*see* photo) *to stay* in the middle of my field not far from the Red Spot. Then she shambled off into the forest only to return in 20 minutes to see her cub again. Then, once more, she left. This coming and going repeated itself half a dozen times over a period of three hours. It had every appearance of a long, sad goodbye. Finally, she left forever! Now was her time to find a gentleman caller—not a hard task I might add.

Little Lady with Pancake Bum

Remarkably, the still-obedient cub stayed in the field until sundown obeying mother's command. It may have stayed hours longer, but I couldn't tell on that moonless night. She[*] was gone in the morning. Now, obedience alone *will not* help her survive although it has taught her many lessons. Life now required a new paradigm. Some learn, some don't; some live, some die. Life's challenge is always the same: adapt or perish.

In her hunger, our young orphan tackled a porcupine—always a poor menu choice (the white arrows show three quills). Unlike some dogs we had on the farm, she will never repeat this mistake. I was cheering for her survival, although almost half of all such castaways die before fall hibernation.

Porcupine Problem

The reader has already realized bears have an amazing physiology. Neither urinating nor defecating, they lie in a dirt hole for five months with no ill effects and no bone loss. Somehow, they reprocess the urea in their urine to create new proteins. I know of no other animal that can do that. Scientists are studying this incredible ability to benefit the bedridden and astronauts both of whom lose considerable bone density from lack of exercise or weightlessness, respectively.

If the fall berry and apple crop should fail and a starvation year ensues, the sow's body will absorb the developing fetuses to preserve her life, nature's birth control. So that winter she will

[*] The cub's small size indicated she was a female.

have no cubs. This unusual phenomenon will synchronize the estrus periods for female bears over the entire crop failure area. I became aware that these periods were in sync in my region.

Because of this phenomenon, the unfortunate little lady with the quills in her face had much competition for food from other orphans. One sow I knew had two large male cubs that she had turned out into the world. Whether she left them at different times or whether they were cast out together, I cannot say. What I do know is I would see one or the other every few days.

Much against the advice of my friends and everyone else, I decided to feed these three orphans with cracked corn and dog kibble. I marvel at the wonders of evolution—this book celebrates its creations—yet that is not a moral or intellectual imperative to imitate its severity. So I stepped in and fed these foundlings who quickly learned to come to my free kitchen several times a day. Both they and I were amply rewarded. The dejected female orphan, who was left in the field, grew into the fine animal pictured standing on the rock pile. She had many cubs of her own in the years that followed. She always brought them to dinner. Clearly, she didn't bring her progeny to show me, but she did manifest a presence and a sense of pride that said, "I, *Ursus americanus*, made these things."

Ego, Ursus americanus, feci haec.

The two male cubs I mentioned earlier finally met at my food kitchen. To me this chance meeting was spectacular for animals that are supposedly solitary. They greeted each other with hugs—yes, bear hugs—and kisses (*see* the "Brothers United"). Their chance encounter was nothing less than joyous. No longer alone and afraid! *Stand by me* they implied to each other, and they did all that summer.

Brothers United

Since they were young and carefree in the forest and the fields, they marched to no drummer but their own. Every day was endless and the summer an eternity. Although they were not in search of moose, wolves, or bears, they did on rare occasions find one. On this fine day, they went into the forest behind my home and turned east toward the rising sun. Perhaps they looked for berries—they were always looking for berries.

CHAPTER—6

MOTHER COURAGE

Our task must be to free ourselves . . . by widening our circle of compassion to embrace all living creatures and the whole of nature and its beauty.
Albert Einstein, Letter reprinted in *The New York Times*, March 29, 1972

Think back to your earliest memory. Now think further back, not to something *you have been told* but to something you actually recall with all its sights, sounds, and smells. My earliest memory, even before that wonderful morning my mother pointed out the doe and her fawn drinking from the lake, was of puppies. It was a rare occasion because my father was actually doing something with me! On an early summer evening, he suggested I go to the horse barn with him. We were in the kitchen at the lumber mill where my mother was busy preparing for tomorrow's breakfast. Three kerosene lanterns hung from crossbeams casting a pale light.

My father took a lantern and we stepped out the screen door into the enveloping darkness where a coterie of moths soon fluttered near the light. In the distance, I could hear the secretive whip-poor-wills calling their name while a chorus of bullfrogs

Whip-poor-will

Bullfrog

from the lake sang "rum, rum, jug-O-rum, rum, rum, rum." It was a short walk to the barn, and, as my dad opened the solid plank door, a pungent odor filled my nostrils. This was a magical place! The placid four-legged giants in their open stanchions were contentedly munching on oats and hay. The faintly lit interior was alive with the power of life: the horses feeding, the barn cat watching mice running across the manger boards, and the moths tickling our faces.

One double stall was empty, and we went up to the manger. While holding the lamp high in his left hand, my father picked me up and held me over the manger that I might see. In the bottom of this crib was a bed of straw cushioning our dog Queenie and her 16 newborn puppies, blind and squirming. To the eyes of a four-year-old, a manger full of puppies is a transcendent experience. Queenie was a gentle and loving animal, and she trusted me when I picked up a puppy and held it to my chest, and ever after in my memory. In a few minutes, my dad put the puppy back and it quickly found a teat and happily nursed. After that perfect moment, I can recall nothing more—as if that memory were so strong, there was room for nothing else.

Everything from that time has vanished: the mill, the cookhouse, the lumber piles, the barns. All the men who worked as machines are gone; my mother and dad are gone. The horses, cats, mice, dogs, and whip-poor-wills are gone. Unless they left progeny, they are meaningless to the genetic history of life on earth. No photographs of these animals, people, or places exist. All this will be forgotten! I have only a sacred memory of a gentle dog in a manger with her puppies, and perhaps, if I write about this remembrance, it may live a little longer.

The next summer we had only one dog from that huge litter of puppies—I dare not reflect on what happened to the others. We called him "Jeff." During those idyllic summer days, Jeff, Queenie, and I were inseparable. The dogs were my only friends, since I was the only child and my mother the only woman at the mill. I particularly loved the beach where I searched for minnows, frogs, crayfish, and clams while the dogs splashed joyously about in the shallow water, and then slept on the warm sand. For reasons unknown, we three friends decided to explore one of the many old logging roads leading to the mill. I would walk in the middle, often with an arm around each dog. Expecting to find new adventures around every turn and over every hill of this rugged path, we walked all morning. This road was not for cars or even trucks but was just the result of horses skidding logs out of the forest to the lake in winter. We walked further. At one point, some partridges boomed out of the undergrowth nearby, but the dogs restrained their natural instincts to stand by me. We walked further. When we were found, according to the men from the mill, we were lost—although I have no recollection that we were. Apparently, when I failed to show up for lunch, Mother in her anxiety had the entire mill shut down and all the workers dispersed to search for me.

When you are with a dog in the forest, you fear no evil; he will be your first line of defense. And what if you have two dogs? These were mongrels, these were hounds, but these were my friends. Until you have loved an animal, a part of your spirit still sleeps.

This has not always been the view of non-human animals. According to the great French philosopher René Descartes (1596–1650), animals are just machines feeling neither pleasure in eating nor pain in suffering. Descartes himself participated in live vivisections on dogs. As English philosopher John Cottingham comments in 1978, "To be able to believe that a dog with a broken paw is not really in pain when it whimpers is a quite extraordinary achievement even for a philosopher." Another Frenchman, Voltaire (1694–1778), agrees:

> Barbarians seize this dog, which in friendship surpasses man so prodigiously; they nail it on a table, and they dissect it alive in order to show the mesenteric veins. You discover in it all the same organs of feeling that are in yourself. Answer me, machinist, has nature arranged all the means of feeling in this animal, so that it may not feel? has it nerves in order to be impassible? Do not suppose this impertinent contradiction in nature.

A decade or so ago, I came upon a considerable mystery. It was a fall afternoon and, while walking down the road toward my home, I couldn't help but notice enormous undulations on the dusty road. A snake perhaps? Now I knew no part of Ontario, or indeed any place on earth, held a snake that huge, at least I hoped not. The S-shaped pattern was approximately 30 inches (76 cm) wide, but its length was uncertain. I thought this thing must swallow deer for breakfast and dine on moose for lunch. My imagination was racing. Adding to the mystery were the occasional patches of dark blood—the remains of prey perhaps?

As the days passed and grew shorter, I often thought about this mystery. What if I ran into this creature on my daily rambles? Eventually the first snow fell overnight, and on that very morning, while checking for animal tracks, I came upon this fantastic winding trail for a second time—and it was close by my home! Once again there were dark bloodstains, this time on pristine snow. Should I be alarmed? I thought not, because anything that large without legs couldn't move quickly. On the other hand, if that were the case, how did this creature capture its prey? My mind was racing again. The mystery deepened when I observed fist-sized footprints in the snow on both sides of the undulations. If I had totally lost my mind, and I wasn't quite there yet, it's possible to imagine this as the serpent from the Garden of Eden. The creature God cursed and made legless to slither on its belly and eat the dust of the earth. In the real world, some snakes, particularly pythons, have vestigial legs as noted in the chapter "A Snake in the Grass." What was happening? How could I solve this enigma?

I have a few additional delusions. In my imagination, I'm a good wildlife photographer, but more interested in the picture's subject than its quality. That is, I would prefer a poor picture of a moose, say, to an award-winning photograph of a landscape. I have cameras that take photographs automatically by sensing both heat and motion. While these *camera traps* take photos, I'm usually at home drinking a Glenmorangie single-malt scotch.

To photograph the extraordinary animal that made these tracks, I attached one of my special cameras to a tree overlooking its trail. I activated it and departed. Days passed, the snow melted, yet nothing happened: no photographs, no new tracks.

I decided this camera trap needed some bait. Feed them and they will come, or so I hoped. Nearby, I placed a large quantity of cracked corn, on the off chance the creature was a herbivore, and four pounds of hamburger in case it was a carnivore—the more likely choice. The following morning I could hardly wait to check the site. As I approached I saw that all the food was gone, every bit of it, and that there were tracks everywhere, including those of this undulating monster. More significantly, the display window on the camera revealed it had taken 186 photographs. Jackpot!

I replaced the memory chip and ran home to boot up my computer to view these pictures. And what did I see? Bears, black bears, lots of them but no undulating monster. One large mother bear or sow came early in the evening with her two small cubs—probably females (*see* picture). Four hours passed before a second mother bear arrived with her two larger cubs—probably males. (Each photograph is imprinted with the date and time it was taken.) But still I saw nothing to explain the strange undulations. What was I missing? I had photographs of the two different sows. Where was the monster?

Large Sow and Her Two Small Female Cubs

Then I saw the problem. The solution to the mystery was obvious, but so incredibly improbable. The mother bear in the next photograph had no use of her hind legs. She was a paraplegic! Note the worn-away fur and exposed flesh on her back legs plus their unnatural position. Unbelievably, *she was dragging herself everywhere*, and this was the source of the undulations.

Mother Courage and Her Two Large Male Cubs

There was no monster, just a mother bear of inconceivable endurance determined to feed her cubs and herself. I decided to call her Mother Courage. There never was a monster, just a delusion in my mind like the bells children sometimes hear in their heads.

I contacted the Ontario Ministry of Natural Resources (MNR) about what we should do to help this injured bear. "We" quickly became "me." But they did suggest that, if this sow made it to hibernation, about two weeks away, the cubs would have a better chance of surviving the winter—it can be 40° below zero where I live. Until then, I decided to feed Mother Courage and her cubs, and to do it outside my back window so that I might observe their behavior. After I began, they came *every night*; however, I never saw the other large sow and her two small cubs again. Two weeks passed, and then two more. Would Mother Courage ever hibernate? I telephoned the MNR to ask if my feeding was inhibiting them from going into hibernation—the officials said not! Another two weeks came and went; it was now the middle of December, and this family often arrived during a blizzard. The cubs were always first by several minutes until this heroic animal dragged her bleeding backside out of the deep forest only to collapse in exhaustion. On many occasions, she never ate—she just watched her cubs devour the cracked corn and dog food. Note the exhausted mother at the back right of the photograph

"Mother Courage Collapsed in Exhaustion" and the concerned cub at the front left. Her mothering instincts could challenge those of most humans.

Mother Courage Collapsed in Exhaustion

I became curious about the location of their wintering den. Because of the broad blood-spotted trail she had imprinted on the snow, I surmised finding her lair would be easy. It must be close; after all, how far can an animal drag itself? Yet it took me more than an hour of arduous scrambling to negotiate my way through a nearly impenetrable tangle of fallen trees and branches. Finally, I reached an embankment sloping down to an ancient glacial lake and located her den (*see* map). This daily journey—both ways—would have intimidated Marco Polo. Yet Mother Courage had done this daily trek for weeks, perhaps even months. I was stunned by the magnitude of her endurance and the power of her instincts. Neither torn flesh, nor exhaustion, nor death itself I thought would prevent her daily rounds. Some will say I am anthropomorphizing; I would say it is simple empathy with a fellow mammal in great anguish—something René Descartes never had.

It's almost impossible to assess an animal's weight accurately by sight alone, but by comparing my first photographs to the later ones, Mother Courage appeared to be losing body fat. So, on December 17, I decided *not to feed* her and her cubs anymore hoping to force them into hibernation, lest she die crawling. It was a melancholy evening for everyone.

They came. They searched. They left. And I never saw them again. Below is the final photograph of that snowy evening.

Mother Courage and Her Children

Early in the New Year, I snowshoed to the den and was elated to find they were all safely asleep—or as asleep as hibernating bears ever truly get. The den entrance was encrusted with ice crystals caused by their emanating body heat. My flashlight revealed the back of a bear almost completely blocking the entrance, perhaps in an effort to retain this heat. I took this to be Mother Courage in her ultimate act of protection for her cubs. She, of course, knew none of this. She was following those deep instincts that had preserved her genes through a million years of evolution.

Clearly, this mother bear was exhibiting behavior that can only be described as *moral*. And just as clearly, this behavior was preserving her genes by enhancing the chance that her two male cubs would survive and reproduce. There was pressure for moral behavior, stemming from natural selection, because this behavior is adaptive for the preservation of genes, which are life itself. In his book *Darwin's Dangerous Idea*, Daniel Dennett calls evolution by natural selection "the best idea anyone has ever had."

A vast literature exists on these topics, not just anecdotal stories such as mine on Mother Courage. Scientists define this topic as follows:

> Sociobiologists believe that human behavior, as well as nonhuman animal behavior, can be partly explained as the outcome of natural selection. They contend that in order to fully understand behavior, it must be analyzed in terms of evolutionary considerations.

At my latitude, 45th parallel north, the average date for bears to come out of hibernation is April 10, so, about two weeks after this date, I revisited the den site. The Ministry of Natural Resources had assured me that this sow (Mother Courage) would not exit the den alive—I had to see for myself. With some difficulty—everything appears different without snow—I found the den again (*see* photo). It was empty, completely empty; the entire family had left. In the distance was a kettle of turkey vultures, and I wondered if they were recycling Mother Courage. I suspected as much, but I declined to investigate.

Empty Bear Den

Male bear cubs will depart from their natal territory—following the instinctive taboo against incest by *Ursus americanus*. Because they leave their home area, they require a larger size, as trespassing on the territories of other male bears (boars) can be hazardous. On occasion they will have to stand and deliver, so it's good to be near or in the same weight division. Genetics tells us that inbreeding is generally detrimental to the gene pool. And, again, natural selection is the source of our discomfort and bears' avoidance of this practice. It's significant that sows will share territory with their female cubs since this sharing presents no danger of incest.

Morality arises in a social context, but even hermits have a need for it in their relationship with nature's wild creatures. All herd or pack animals have a large moral repertoire: whales, elephants, and, as we shall see, wolves.

Algonquin Wolf   Algonquin Wolf at Night

In Western society, if you wish to conjure up a nightmare of slobbering immorality, of heartless cruelty and mindless killing, the image is always that of the wolf. From nursery rhymes to adult fiction, the beast from the primeval forest is *Canis lupus lupus*. Never was a creature more maligned than this great grandparent of *Canis lupus familiaris*, the family pet. Yet there are only two authenticated cases of *wild* wolves killing humans as prey in all of North American recorded history.

On the other hand, we have poisoned, trapped, and slaughtered so many wolves—running them down with snowmobiles and shooting from helicopters—that they are virtually extirpated from the lower forty-eight states. Under great protest, a few have been reintroduced to Yellowstone Park. Often, though, we know who the top predator is, the slobbering mindless killer—we need only look in the mirror.

Experts have long thought wolf-pack size was determined solely by the abundance of food. In my region the average pack of five or six wolves hunts over an area of approximately 100 square miles (260 km^2). Yet even in the presence of an overabundance of prey, pack size is relatively fixed. Why? All species of wolves live in tight-knit social groups. If the pack grows too large, the group disintegrates because members are not able to bond closely enough with each other. Curiously, the number of relationships grows more quickly than the actual pack size. In a pack of five there are ten relationships; however, in a pack of ten this number jumps to forty-five—far too many for close bonding. The chart below shows how quickly the number of relationships rises in proportion to the pack size:

Pack Size	1	2	3	4	5	6	7	8	9	10
Number of Relationships	0	1	3	6	10	15	21	28	36	45

The common paradigm for wolf behavior comes from Tennyson's *In Memoriam*, which calls nature's final law "red in tooth and claw." But if this were true of wolves, the pack would quickly disintegrate from animosity, injury, and death. You cannot risk your life every day or you will soon lose it. Approximately 90 per cent of wolf-pack interactions are prosocial. That is not to say that wolves, like our military or our entire social order, don't have a strict hierarchy, which accounts for the remaining 10 percent.

In social groups with a hierarchical structure, a method is needed to release the tension caused by the restrictions on freedom. Ancient Rome developed the yearly feast of Saturnalia when masters served slaves. To be sure the slaves, nonetheless, prepared the food. Wolves have an analogous game in which the dominant individuals "handicap" themselves in role reversals with lower ranking wolves by showing submission and permitting them to play bite. If a wolf bites too hard, it will "play bow" to ask forgiveness, and the play resumes. This is a clear demonstration of fairness, so pack tensions are released and bonding is reinforced.

Unlike the Romans indulging only during the Saturnalia, which was a yearly festival, wolves play fight regularly throughout the year. Their bonds are tightly knit and compassionate especially around any newborn pups, to whom every wolf is a parent of sorts: older siblings from previous litters, aunts, and uncles. If the alpha female happens to die giving birth or otherwise, various aunts will care for the young, and these females will even lactate.

Marc Bekoff, Professor Emeritus of Ecology and Evolutionary Biology at the University of Colorado, claims that, without a moral code governing their actions, animals could not exhibit these kinds of behaviors. With co-author Jessica Pierce, bioethicist, Bekoff cogently argues this point in the book *Wild Justice: The Moral Lives of Animals*.

Naturally, moral differences exist between humans and other animals just as they do among all individuals of the same species including *Homo sapiens*. It's a matter of degree not of kind.

Many readers may have wondered how Mother Courage came to be a paraplegic. Only two reasonable speculations are possible: she was either hit by a car[*] or shot by a hunter. It was bear hunting season when I first noticed the undulations on my dusty road. Hunting or "harvesting," as the euphemism goes, is from 1 September until hibernation—almost three months. However, "harvesting" season on humans is always closed. All biology textbooks describe bears as "shy woodland creatures," and they are very rarely dangerous to humans. In this century, the number of people killed by a mother bear defending her cubs can be counted on the fingers of one hand. And most died as the result of being mauled, so, when it comes to protecting their young, we can say of bears mauling yes, killing no.

World black bear expert Lynn Rogers says the following on his website (www.bear.org):

> Black bears have killed 61 people across North America since 1900. This no longer worries me. My chances of being killed by a domestic dog, bees, or lightning are vastly greater. My chances of being murdered are 60,000 times greater. One of the safest places a person can be is in the woods.

[*] *See* Chapter 5 "Bears, Oh My!"

Humans, however, have slaughtered hundreds of thousands of bears. We hunt bears, bears do not hunt us.

With our so-called God-given morality, we have driven hundreds if not thousands of species to extinction, and another universe must pass away before such creatures will ever come again. Remember the Bible tells us God gave us dominion over all life and we have taken it with a vengeance. I am not a vegetarian, but I would speak against the *senseless* slaughter of all those who cannot speak for themselves.

> *A dog starved at his Masters Gate*
> *Predicts the ruin of the State*
> William Blake, "Auguries of Innocence" (c. 1803) 1.9–10

Some moral behaviors exist outside of, and independent of, humans. Even among those who didn't hear Moses fresh back from Sinai where God gave him *another two tablets* and said call me in the morning[*]! If as a species, we had never existed or had gone extinct—and 99 percent of all species have—morality in terms we could recognize would still be flourishing on this planet.

The most fascinating behavior between animals—human or otherwise—is reciprocity. You scratch my back and I'll scratch yours. Or, unexpectedly, I'll scratch yours even if I don't know you or will never see you again. Another name for reciprocity is the Golden Rule. Nonetheless, animals had it first, long before the Bible reiterated it, or Moses staggered down Mount Sinai in a rage.

To the shock of those who are stony faced and stony minded, the evidence that humans, apes and monkeys, whales, elephants, wolves, and even rats and mice inherit ethical behaviors honed by natural selection is profoundly disturbing. But should it be? We are a part *of*, not apart *from*, all life on earth. We are not descended from angels but ascended from apes. Ours is a heroic past, at times so close to extinction that a wink might have made it so. Darwin would be pleased to witness the expansion of morality to non-human animals by natural selection.

---

[*] R_x swallow whole; do not smash. Repeats: 0

Only a single *verified* theory of evolution exists. Previous competitors have all been vanquished in the marketplace of ideas—Lamarckism from France, Lysenkoism from the former Soviet Union, and creationism from America are three such fallen warriors. Darwin's theory of evolution by natural selection stands alone, undefeated and now unchallenged. Since its historic publication in 1859, *On the Origin of Species* has continued to gather strength and verification from related branches of science. It is now firmly established as one of the greatest ideas of all time and as certain as heliocentricism.

Thousands of creation myths exist. Even the Torah has two: the first in Genesis 1, the second in Genesis 2. None of these tall tales agree in the fine print. Creationism isn't a theory with proof; it's a theory with poof. In the beginning there was no universe, then God said, "*POOF*," and there it was.

Darwinian evolution is like chemistry, physics, and mathematics in that it works everywhere on Earth, Mars, and the far reaches of the universe, even as far as Kansas. Instead creationism, creation science, or intelligent design, or whatever it's called now, is parochial. People sometimes say to me that *I believe* in evolution just as *they believe* in creationism. To any rational person it is not a matter of belief. Any examination of the evidence will compel a reasonable person to accept evolution.

Acceptance of evolution solely because of the evidence and not because of society's beliefs is a bellwether of how well a civilization is thriving. Show me a nation that rejects evolution on the basis of ideology, and I'll show you a society in trouble. At least 40 percent of the adult US population believes evolution is false, and another 20 percent is confused about the issue. American creationists have their bedfellows in Iran, Iraq, Afghanistan, Jordan, Saudi Arabia, the Emirates, Turkey, Yemen, Somalia, Syria, and so on. These are their intellectual equals. Borat, aka Sacha Baron Cohen, has fun with creationism in his famous poster. The translation reads as follows, "Cultural Learnings of Darwood [Darwin] for Make Benefit Glorious Notion of Creationism."

POSTSCRIPT: I knew Mother Courage before she had that name. She was the little orphan with the porcupine quills in her face and a hunger in her belly. Her distinguishing mark was that she had none; her coat was a beautiful black sheen. Many bears have a white chevron on their chests of varying sizes and symmetry— Barney had one. Another young male bear I knew had such a prominent and perfect mark that I nicknamed him "Chevy."

Stand and Deliver

When she was a cub and a young mother, I would see Mother Courage almost every summer day. We were acquaintances, so neither of us feared the other. This near friendship started shortly after she became an orphan. It was sealed the sunny afternoon she ventured onto my deck in search of seeds spilled from my bird feeders. When I first noticed her, she was sitting on the deck's railing looking directly at me as if to say, "Food, please."

Instantly I grabbed my camera, and ever so slowly, I opened the door. The orphan seemed mesmerized yet held her position. Finally, I had the door opened far enough to get a few clear photos. The reader should note that, in her anxiety, the cub peed on the railing, but she stood her ground. We are all afraid but some can control their fear, and this discipline became her defining feature. Even at an early age, she was a unique animal because most bears would have instantly disappeared into the forest. On this day our relationship began; from here, it continued to its tragic end.

Pole Dancing

I knew her as a cub, teenager, young adult, mother, and finally as a paraplegic. My three favorite pictures are the pole dance photograph and the two below, which were taken at the beginning and end of her life.   In the next picture, she is resting in my sunny orchard waiting for me to serve dinner.

Young in My Fields

In the photograph taken on a bleak November night, she is just hanging on to life. But, in my mind's eye, Mother Courage will always be the bravest and most enduring creature I have ever known.

Old in a Twisted Body

Do not go gentle into that good night.
Rage, rage against the dying of the light.
Dylan Thomas

CHAPTER—7

THE FOX KNOWS

And green and golden I was huntsman and herdsman, the calves
Sang to my horn, the foxes on the hills barked clear and cold...
Dylan Thomas, "Fern Hill"

Wintertime and the living is hard. Reynard is on the prowl. Because of the deep snow, he hasn't hunted in two days. It's – 40°; the red glow of dawn fills the east as he meanders through a field of wisteria bushes and poplar saplings. Reynard has no destination, he's going nowhere, and everywhere—this is the hunt. It's the prey that's important, not his location; he follows his ears, nose, and eyes. Since the snow is deep, he treads with great care *conserving energy* however possible. His track pattern is unusual for a four-legged animal: he leaves only half the expected paw prints. His smaller hind paw lands in the impression just made by the front paw on the same side. That is, he "double prints," as we do

through deep snow when following a friend because it's less arduous. Reynard dreams of mice and voles or perhaps a plump partridge sleeping in its overnight snow cave. He hasn't eaten in two days.

To conserve energy in snow, many other animals such as wolves and coyotes also double print. Artificial selection and a full food bowl have rendered dogs incapable of doing so—they commonly make a four-print pattern. Through a hundred thousand years, natural selection pressures have favored energy-conserving behaviors. In a million-year march, a minuscule pebble in a boot can be crippling.

Fox Double Printing

You will discover these energy-saving behaviors, these max-imizing and minimizing activities, across the entire spectrum of life. Often they're subtle, usually they're overlooked, but they're always necessary for long-term survival. Consider the humble bumblebee. Bernd Heinrich in his lucid and lively book *Bumble-bee Economics* reveals their innumerable adaptive behaviors. On a summer's day, in the same field of wisteria where Reynard conducted his winter hunt you can see bumblebees going about their tasks. Here's one survival adaptation Heinrich notes:

> The wider resources are scattered, the less efficient it is to re-cruit and defend specific items, and the more difficult it is to patrol and defend an area. Competitors then appear to work peacefully (without contact) side by side, but they may still compete relentlessly by trying to remove resources faster than the next individual. Aggressive encounters then become a liabil-ity, for even the winners lose—they have only expended time and energy that could have been used for foraging. The nonag-gressors, which do not interrupt their foraging, reap more food energy and are competitively superior. Such competition, called scramble or exploitation competition, generally results in the depletion of resources to the very minimum of economic profit-ability. In turn, it selects for energy economy and foraging effi-ciency in the contestants.

Two Species of Bumblebee Scramble

This is *natural selection* at work, at all times, in all places—even as you read. As the greatest evolutionary geneticist of our time, Theodosius Dobzhansky writes, "Nothing in biology makes sense except in the light of evolution."

Although, as I have mentioned, my cousin and I were not in search of moose, bears, or wolves, we were, however, always looking for foxes. The fox is the most cat-like of the canids (the dog family). When my cousin and I were young, we discovered a fox den with kits in a field gently sloping down to a small lake some distance from our farm. To watch their behaviors, we hid in a wooded hillside above the den. The vixen (mother fox) never saw us, and her ever-playful pups didn't care. Their bright red

Can You Come Out to Play?

coats and white-tipped tails stood out against the yellow and brown of the field making them easy to see. In those days, we had no eagles so an aerial attack was unlikely, and their den was nearby. Often we saw only the kits; the vixen and the dog fox (male) were away catching mice, squirrels, and rabbits for their ravenous youngsters.

As we hid on the hillside, we were quiet and attentive to the theater below. The pups, however, were anything but; they jumped, tumbled, and ran continuously. This field by the lake was their schoolyard where they played and prepared, on the edge of adulthood, practicing those energy-saving behaviors noted previously. To correct Descartes "they play, therefore they were!" At our distance, we could just hear their playful yelps and squeals. Otherwise, everything was quiet; time seemed imperceptible as the sunny field jumped with life, and these sprightly red balls ran their heedless ways. The vixen and dog fox had fulfilled their genetic obligations, and their genes are most likely still running through these same fields although the watchers no longer watch.

I now realize my cousin and I were young foxes with our needs provided for by laboring, loving, and uncomplaining adults. These adults piled the thousands of stones into rock fences and fashioned hand-hewn boards into houses and stacked logs into barns while pushing their fists into the rocky soil to pull out a living. And all the while, we ran our heedless ways. For us the sun was born over and over anew each day. We played, therefore we were!

The Breaker of Backs

Decades later, when I lived in my home beside the Red Spot, many things had changed; it was a new generation. The fields were going back to nature, and photographing the same field a decade apart will affirm this transformation. At first, the changes are almost imperceptible but they accelerate rapidly over time. Red, black, and choke cherries were immigrants and are now so large that in mast years feasting bears often fall out of these trees* in front of me before bolting into the forest. It's exhilarating!

On a June morning while on one of my many rambles, I noticed a vertical reddish strip at some distance. Turning my binoculars on this object, I confirmed it was a fox standing on its hind legs observing me. I wondered why? I soon discovered the answer. The fox left and I continued toward the old barn; within 50 paces, the answer appeared. A family of five fox pups was living under the barn. They were playing, of course, but since I was close, they noticed me and scurried back to their basement apartment. I waited. Within a few minutes, the bravest, or most foolish, kit poked his head out to look directly at me. I didn't move. He became bolder and was soon followed by his more cautious litter mates. It was a marvelous private showing, one that conjured up remembrances of times past.

Peek, I See You

---

* I tend to walk looking down rather than up; at times, this can be a problem.

Porcupine under the Barn

That evening I reflected on the barn's new non-paying tenants, and quickly realized this old house was filled with freeloaders. The structure that once housed horses and cows now had new residents who just wandered in from the forest and sky. At the diagonally opposite corner to the foxes, lives an old bachelor porcupine carrying his evolution on his back, not far away from a young woodchuck too lazy to do his only trick and dig a burrow. And in every vacant basement apartment, you will find snowshoe hares. In the higher stories, there are raccoons, flying squirrels, chipmunks, and mice, of course, lots of mice, voles, moles, and shrews. I feel certain milk snakes still rest on the 60-year-old hay watching for rodents. A few years ago, when several sheets of metal roofing blew off in a storm, access to the hayloft became available for turkey vultures to nest. Now eastern phoebes build nests under the barn's eves while bumblebees make a home in abandoned mouse nests. Nature finds a way to reuse old habitats. At the peak of each gable end on the barn, my grandfather cut pentagonal openings for barn swallows to enter and nest, but they have not returned for many years and I miss them.

Foxes are mostly nocturnal and extremely skittish, more so even than wolves. It's not a stretch to imagine that those not so wary have been selected out of the population, that they've been shot, trapped, and poisoned. Yes, we humans have been responsible for some aspects of wolf and fox evolution. The discharge of a rifle will send many species, including my dog, scattering for safety—and wisely so.

On occasion in winter, I collect road-kill deer and put the carcasses in my fields for recycling. A carcass attracts a whole spectrum of birds and mammals for me to view and photograph. Feed them and they will come! There is nothing ignoble in a large predator scavenging—be it eagle, bear, wolf, or fox. Certainly early man did the same. Life dances precariously on the edge between maximizing resources and death, and early humans heard that drum beat and knew that hunger. But since the agricultural revolution brought humans a great abundance of food, many have forgotten our hunter-gatherer-scavenger roots.

Chow Down on Deer Carcass

Foxes are frequent visitors to my roadkill offerings. The incredible contrast of the fox's coat with the snow couldn't be more extreme. Surely, his color and the fact that his eyes are shielded makes him a perfect target for eagles—which are now abundant and also come to my free feast. Perhaps with plenty of easy food, the eagle at the deer carcass (*see* photo) wisely

American Bald Eagle at Deer Carcass

decides not to attack the scrappy fox, and the fox, well, the fox knows many things.

As a short aside, let me mention our hunter-gatherer-scavenger ancestors, and how they adapted to their changing environments. Consider that, when we first came out of the trees onto the African savannah, like the fox that watched me near the barn, we stood on our hind legs to see over the tall grasses for predators and prey. Standing upright also reduces the heat (sunlight) falling on the body, a distinct advance in persistence hunting. Conservation is our future; hunting was our past. Consider this past:

> It's dark. Although the first gray mists of morning fill the east, sunrise seems a long way off as you huddle in the cold rocks with your fellow hunter-gatherers. From the plain below the nocturnal roars of the predators and the cries of their prey fill you with terror. This is the second night on the same hillock. The previous dawn a pride of lions killed a wildebeest at the base of the rocks; they feasted all morning. After that, the jackals and vultures took what was left as the lions rested under a nearby acacia tree.
>
> The quickly rising sun was about to break over the eastern ridge and the roar of lions could still be heard in the distance. One old male returned to the bare bones of the beast in the hope of finding a forgotten fragment. Finally, the moment has come, and with the sun shining full on your face, you and your friends break like a whirlwind from the rocks in an all-out running assault on the male lion. Your numbers, and the stones and sticks you carry, chase him from the standing rib cage. You don't slacken your pace until you reach the worthless prize. Even though you have driven the lion away, it seems you're a day late. But one of the older men takes a large wildebeest femur, places it on a flat rock, and smashes it with another rock. It splits revealing the rich marrow within—the prize you have been waiting for. Only wolverines, hyenas, and some wolves can crush bones with their jaws and reach this precious food source. Man does it with his brain. Welcome to the world of ideas!

Humans adapt *by culture and construction*; non-humans adapt *mostly by bodily changes*. This ability to affect the environment is our advantage: it allows us to live on every continent, in space, and on the moon. Yet for all other species, an environment that changes too quickly for their bodies to adapt is a death sentence.

This view of humans is expressed eloquently in the first paragraph of Jacob Bronowski's magnificent book and TV series *The Ascent of Man*:

> Man is a singular creature. He has a set of gifts which make him unique among the animals: so that, unlike them, he is not a figure in the landscape—he is a shaper of the landscape. In body and in mind he is the explorer of nature, the ubiquitous animal, who did not find but has made his home in every continent.

Now, in no way do I wish to deny how remarkable humans are (*see* last chapter), but, if you change just three things (indicated in red), the Bronowski quotation applies equally well to the fox.

> The fox is a singular creature. He has a set of gifts which make him unique among the animals: so that, unlike them, he is not a figure in the landscape—he is a master of the landscape. In body and in mind he is the explorer of nature, the ubiquitous animal, who did not find but has made his home in every continent, except Antarctica.

The Master of His Landscape

The red fox is the world's most widely distributed carnivore. And a species of foxlike animal existed until 1876 on the Falkland Islands, part of the Antarctic biosystem. It's still a mystery how they got there, although scientists now believe their ancestors probably chased penguins and seals across the frozen sea.

Warrah—the Foxlike Falkland Islands Wolf

On his five-year voyage around the world on the *HMS Beagle*, Charles Darwin visited the Falklands. He was amazed to find these isolated islands had a foxlike canid with the classic white-tipped tail, that the locals called the warrah. Before the Welsh and Scottish immigrants colonized these islands, they were uninhabited, and hence the warrah had developed no fear of humans—a costly trait. The Falklands may have had two different species of this canid. Darwin—always the close observer— wrote that the warrahs of the West and East Falkland Islands were but variants that differed depending on which island they came from:

> When I see these Islands in sight of each other, & possessed of but a scanty stock of animals, tenanted by these birds but slightly differing in structure & filling the same place in Nature, I must suspect they are only varieties. The only fact of a similar kind of which I am aware is the constant asserted difference between the wolf-like Fox of East & West Falkland Islands. If there is the slightest foundation for these remarks the zoology of Archipelagoes will be well worth examining; for such facts undermine the stability of Species.

The Falklands with its warrahs had all ingredients of what Darwin later found on the Galapagos Islands with its tortoises and finches. And in the next chapter, we will consider his finches of the Galapagos and ours of the great northern forests.

If you wander the forests and fields of any land, you will soon find death. It comes in the form of the rigid bodies of those who have left us. Dylan Thomas says it touchingly when he describes, in *A Child's Christmas in Wales*, his search "for news of the little world": he would "find always a dead bird . . . perhaps a robin, all but one of his fires out."

Before my cousin and I found the dead bear and removed its eyeteeth, we had discovered other fatalities: mice, partridge, turtles, snakes, frogs, but rarely small birds, I suspect scavengers had run off with the latter. In recent years, I have located moose and deer carcasses from wolf kills, wings of hawks, headless snakes, dead kangaroo mice, weasels, raccoons, and porcupines. The dead litter this land. You cannot lie down anywhere in the forests or the fields without resting on the graves of the fallen. Even my cousin is buried near my home, as was his mother's wish.

The main engine of evolution is death. Death powers Life. If we were immortals, evolution would not exist. Only by the passing of the possibly less well adapted, which leaves space and food for others, can the next generation test its genes.

One of my remote cameras photographed a fox on a road-killed deer that I had left in the forest. A close examination revealed he had lost his symmetry and, with it, much of his health and vigor: I noted his "crunched face" and awkward left hind leg. One of life's contingencies had befallen him, perhaps an injury in a scrap over a vixen resulting in a systemic infection, but I guess at what I do not know.

The very next day when I returned to check my camera, this fox was dead on my snowshoe trail where the walking was easiest. He had collapsed on his left side, but his right legs were still in stride. He died walking not after 10,000 steps, but probably 100,000 strides that morning. In unavoidable sympathy, I marveled at his endurance, and only hoped I would do as well.

It took some effort, but as a gesture of respect, I buried him where he fell. So that the next summer he might become a wild-flower, then a rabbit, and finally a fox. Although he is not im-mortal, he will have life everlasting and forever run on through the evergreen forests and the wisteria fields in his eternal pursuit of food.

The Red Fox—All But One of His Fires Out

All creatures great and small of the living world must practice an economy, whose purpose is to stay alive and pass on genes. We have seen this in Reynard's double printing, the bumblebee's dedication to the work ethic, and the reflective layer on the reti-nas of nocturnal mammals (*see* chapter on wolves). At a deep level, chemistry and physics make the rules that life dances to. If your niche is the water's skin, like the whirligig bug, you dare not gain too much weight, lose too many legs, or sharpen your nails. Charles Darwin wrote the book on the innumerable minor rules of survival and the one supreme principle, *natural selection.*

It's later now, the sun is up, but a light snow is beginning to fall while Reynard hunts on. As one of his many survival strategies, he caches food. Earlier, he had retrieved a previously hidden red squirrel; it made a nice snack and has fueled his body. Like the lemmings that his arctic cousins devour in great numbers, the meadow voles in this field of wisteria go through high and low cycles, and this is a low year. Nevertheless, Reynard hears a subnivean vole seven body lengths away; he creeps closer, but not so close as to alert the ever-vigilant prey. The fox and the vole have been playing their evolutionary game for eons. Each has helped to shape what the other has become, and they are still engaged in this evolutionary contest, a tournament worthy of the mettle of both.

Here's the dilemma for Reynard. He must eat voles to live, yet he can't approach them because the least sound—the snap of a twig, the crackle of a leaf, or the crunch of compressed snow—sends the creature scurrying away into its network of tunnels. The solution: do a standing long jump from as far away as possible. He must launch himself like a rocket, bullet, or football; the physics is the same, discovered by Galileo and explained in his famous *Dialogue on the Great World Systems.* Just five factors determine the range (distance) of any projectile whatsoever, and on this planet, we have no control over one of these—gravity. So the remaining four decide how far foxes can jump, and within these, Reynard follows great evolution and science:

- The weight—foxes are the lightest of the canids.
- The length of time this force is applied—foxes have the longest hind legs of related dog-like carnivores.
- The muscular force exerted on the ground before flight.
- The angle—the fox must find the one that maximizes his range.

At any given time, however, he is unable to significantly alter the first three of these factors: his weight and the *power* of the exerted force—the latter is determined by the length and strength of his hind legs. So these four conditions reduce to one, the angle of launch. This was a classic problem of early ballistics. The angle required for the greatest range is the same for all projectiles be they living or dead, pigskin or rock, frog or fox. It's 45°—*see* the diagram. For Reynard, every day is another Olympic event; jumps must be swift, high, and strong.

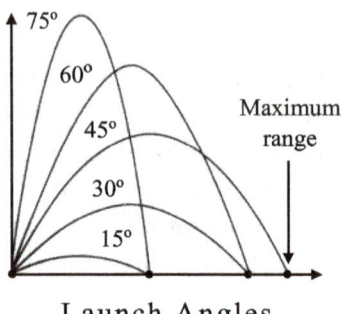

Launch Angles

Observation of foxes shows they do use an angle very close to 45°. However, if the snow cover is firm and a greater downward force is required to trap the vole, then the angle is higher, lower if the snow is soft. Through practice, Reynard knows the geometry of range and impact, that the sum of these angles adds up to 90 degrees.

Why does Reynard lunge? To catch voles of course. He's the ultimate mousetrap, but there is more to it than that. Scientists have been in a long retreat from earlier denials of all human feelings to other creatures, ascribing every animal behavior to instinct.

The Fox Knows Many Things

But I believe Reynard also lunges for the thrill of it! His ember-colored body soars in an exciting graceful parabola to land exactly on his supper. The fox knows many things; the woodchuck knows only one.

CHAPTER—8

THE SEED WARRIORS

And this our life, exempt from public haunt,
Finds tongues in trees, books in the running brooks,
Sermons in stones, and good in everything.
Shakespeare, *As You Like It*

W e left the farm when I was five, and moved to the city to live with one of my mother's sisters. As I learned later, there were two reasons for this move: so my parents could find work and I could attend school. My mother was sympathetic toward my desire to return to the farm, so every Dominion Day she took me back to paradise for July and August, the summer months.

After the age of six, I spent the rest of the year in the city attending school so, I saw no winter birds, nor did I know any. Besides, in those days no one I knew had bird feeders, they were too busy trying to feed themselves and their families. All that was about to change!

Pine Grosbeak in Snowstorm

After World War I, my grandfather purchased the adjoining 100-acre "farm" and gave the original homestead to his only son. It's on this second farm, with its vast system of barns and five-bedroom home with two staircases, that my cousin and I spent so many blissful days. As mentioned in the chapter on turkeys, I eventually purchased the "back 40" of this second farm and built a cabin and ultimately a house near the Red Spot. My home is within sight of the original barn and its host of new residents.

It was January and I was snowshoeing by myself up through this second farm (my uncle's) whose buildings exist now only in my memory and in few faded photographs. It felt lonely and strangely unfriendly although there was no wind and the snowflakes were large and falling slowly. I could have been on the tundra—everything was gray and deadly quiet. As I ascended the hill to where the barnyard once sat, I could hear my heart beating. Looking around I recognized nothing but the double balsam fir tree my uncle had planted. I turned down what I thought was the path to the spring field, the field my cousin and I had so often retrieved the turkeys from to return them to the safety of the barns. The snow became heavier, but fortunately, I recognized another tree and a fence. I wasn't lost, at least not yet. The piercing silence and the monotone grayness were gloomy and depressive. "Perk up," I told myself. "In less than an hour you'll be

Male (top) and Female (bottom) Pine Grosbeaks

inside your snug cabin with a warm fire and supper cooking on the stove." Now I was in the middle of the spring field, so I turned sharply toward the east and my cabin.

It was then that I first heard the solid high-pitched chirps and saw a very large object directly in front of me through the grayness of the fading light and the falling snow. I stopped abruptly! It stopped also. A moose perhaps? It still didn't move. Again, I heard the high-pitched chirps, and, at that moment, something flew by my head! Incredibly, it was a flock of a dozen or so birds, and they landed in the large object directly in front of me—a tree. As I approached the tree, I could see these astonishingly red birds removing the "flesh" of its small crab apples to get at the five black seeds in the core. For efficiency, they removed only half the fruit, revealing the tiny black prizes.

Flock of Pine Grosbeaks

This was an old tree and I recognized its three-trunk form and twisted torso. In the summer months, my cousin and I eagerly devoured its sweet apples, but we spat out the core unlike these hardy birds. I stood there in wonder at their beauty in this cold, dreary, gray landscape and my spirit ascended. These red warriors were fearless. I was now within an arm's length, yet they completely ignored me. For some 20 minutes, I watched this show until all the apples were filleted. Then, suddenly, the entire flock took wing, privy to a signal I did not know.

Monarch of the Great Northern Forests

I learned these birds were pine grosbeaks, a large finch of the circumpolar forests—wanderers across the vastness of North America, Siberia, European Russia, and Scandinavian, searchers of pine seeds, apple cores, and mountain ash berries. Their closest relative is the crimson-browed finch of the Himalayan Mountains. Like the warrahs of the Falkland Islands, they rarely see humans; hence they are fearless.

> *Bird, bird, burning bright,*
> *In the forests of the night;*
> *What immortal hand or eye,*
> *Could frame thy gorgeous symmetry?*

I hope William Blake will forgive my mischief with his famous lines. But what immortal hand or eye has framed this gorgeous symmetry? The females and the similarly colored juveniles blend easily into the forest. The coloring of the males gives no quarter to camouflage, and it's clearly harmful to their individual survival. It seems to say, "Here I am, red on white, catch me if you can!" Why such foolish advertising? Charles Darwin knew to what end such beauty exists: the females found red *sexually attractive* and a sign of good health. These seldom seen firebirds are as stunning as any painting ever created. In comparison, Renaissance masters should weep over their dull

Charles Darwin

creations. Why do males continue to face such dangers? Only those attractive enough to find a mate pass on their genes. The great naturalist named the process *sexual selection.* Females almost exclusively determine the rules. If they prefer male birds with longer tails or brighter colors, the lucky fellows with these traits will become fathers. And their male progeny will likely be even more attractive to the ladies than dad was. Darwin conjectured that the male beard, as well as the relative hairlessness of humans compared to other mammals, resulted from sexual selection. This hairlessness trait is in full force today in Western society—not so much elsewhere.

The pine grosbeak is not the only large finch of the great boreal forests. While building my cabin—about the size of Thoreau's at Walden Pond—I saw my first evening grosbeak. It was November and snowing, of course, and my cousin and I were putting the final row of shingles on the roof. I don't remember if he was sweeping the snow away as I nailed the shingles or the reverse. But at some point, a half-dozen of these noisy parrot-like birds landed in the sugar maple tree beside the cabin.

Evening Grosbeak

It almost seemed as if they were asking us to feed them. My *Peterson's Field Guide to the Birds* quickly confirmed they were evening grosbeaks. Neither of us had previously seen these birds, and, in fact, they were recent immigrants to Ontario.

I did feed them, not that day but for decades to come. And they in turn awarded me their noisy abundance and robust scrappiness. To see a flock of 200 swirl out of the snow and the sky to descend on your feeder is an exhilarating experience. After those abundant years when I was young, their numbers severely declined to the original half-dozen of a snowy day in November.

The gross beaks I have just described are not grosbeaks but rather finches with extra-large bills. Experts classify true finches by the number of wing feathers (12) and the number of primary tail feathers (9). Normally, though, we don't have the option of counting today. Gone—happily—are the days of Audubon and Darwin, when we shot birds to identify them properly. Today we identify a flock of finches by their undulating flight, notched tails, and distinctive calls.

The world's most famous finches are those collected by Darwin and his *servant* Syms Covington* on the Galapagos Islands. Darwin thought they were blackbirds, grosbeaks, and finches. Following Darwin's return to England, the famous ornithologist John Gould said they were all finches. Further research led Gould to conclude this new grouping included 15 different species. Here are four with the greatest range in beak size:

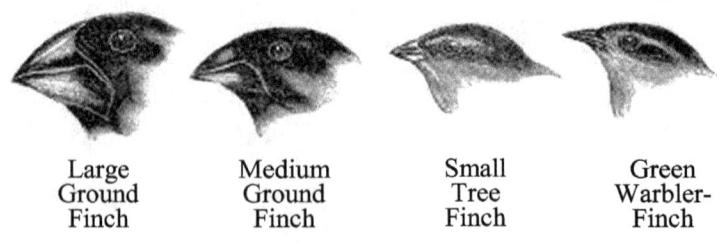

| Large Ground Finch | Medium Ground Finch | Small Tree Finch | Green Warbler-Finch |

---

* *See Mr. Darwin's Shooter: A Novel* by Roger McDonald for an interesting but mostly fictional biography of Covington.

These birds have little or nothing that attracts the eye being all brown or black. They are fit companions to the marine iguanas of the Galapagos that Darwin called the "imps of darkness." It wasn't until Darwin was back in England that the significance of these finches became apparent. While in the Galapagos, he was mainly interested in geology, so he neglected to label which island his finches came from. Covington collected finches for himself, but he labeled the island of origin for each bird. Upon Darwin's request, his faithful assistant passed this crucial information along to his master. It proved to be enormously significant!

Syms Covington

At the age of 15, Covington went to sea as a cabin boy and fiddler on board the *HMS Beagle* during her voyage around the world. Captain Robert Fitzroy appointed him to assist Charles Darwin and be his personal servant—a position he retained after their return to England.

To be sure, there was the unavoidable air of an upstairs-downstairs relationship between these young men. Darwin's father was a doctor with a house full of servants while Covington's father worked in a slaughterhouse and had a house full of children. With some truth, we could say that the assistant provided the data that the master wove into his great theory. Yet nowhere in any of Darwin's books is Covington mentioned by name; he is called "my servant," a designation Covington detested. Probably to escape this caste system, he immigrated to Australia, married, and had eight children. When his copy of *On the Origin of Species* arrived, Covington must have been disappointed that his name was not mentioned. His tombstone in Pambula, New South Wales, correctly and proudly announces him as the "Assistant to Charles Darwin."

Nevertheless, these men were friends. Darwin gave his assistant a letter of recommendation when Covington sailed for Australia. And, because Covington developed a hearing problem during the voyage of the *Beagle*, Darwin later gave him an ear trumpet. In turn, Covington sent Darwin some unusual barnacles from the southern continent.

Beginning in 1846, the famous naturalist had a love affair with barnacles and spent eight years in their service, work that resulted in four volumes listing all known types around the world. The study of these creatures so dominated the Darwin household that his son Francis would famously ask of another child, "Where does your father do his barnacles?"

Those snowy November days my cousin and I spent roofing my cabin were the last we would be together for weeks at a time. After that both he and I married, worked, had children, worked, eventually divorced, and worked. On occasion, we would get together for an afternoon or evening and reminisce on the days of our youth. We never talked about evolution. I thought it wasn't part of his universe, but I was mistaken. On the other hand, he somehow knew Darwin's dangerous idea held a world of wonders for me.

One evening while we were drinking a single-malt scotch, he opened his wallet and removed a faded newspaper clipping as if to reveal some hidden secret to me. I read it. He had been carrying around a news item recounting the false tale of Darwin's deathbed recanting of his theory and last-minute embrace of religion. I was stunned and quickly realized how far our worlds had drifted apart since those halcyon summer days. We talked! We disagreed! And we never mentioned it again.

Had I known then what I know now about our northern finches, perhaps he could have been persuaded. I doubt, however, that Darwin's ugly birds would have meant anything to him. Here are *all eight* beautiful northern finches arranged roughly in order of beak size:

Evening Grosbeak   Purple Finch

Red Crossbill   White-Winged Crossbill

Pine Grosbeak   Pine Siskin

American Goldfinch   Redpoll

Both the red and the white-winged crossbill adapt not by beak *size* but by beak *shape*. Their strangely crossed bills appear to be a deformity. At first, critics of Darwinism—and they are everywhere—were delighted with this presumed evolutionary blunder. But the essence of *descent with modification*, Darwin's preferred phrase, is that poor designs are selected out, and quickly.

Extracting seeds from tight pinecones is no easy task, and the crossed bill is uniquely suited to this job. The bird inserts its sharply pointed beak under a pinecone's scale then moves the bill's top and bottom sections further apart to extract the seed with its long tongue, thousands per day—a spectacular adaptation

Male Red Crossbill

for a difficult task*. If the cone crop is extensive, crossbills will nest and feed their babies using this "evolutionary blunder" even in January.

Of these eight finches, only one was commonly seen on the farm during the summer months, the American goldfinch, colloquially known as the wild canary. My cousin and I would see them most evenings grasping one of the wires of our endless clotheslines.

American Goldfinch on Scotch Thistle

---

* *See* Cornell University's video http://biology.allaboutbirds.org/white-winged-crossbill-foraging-adaptation/

They are late nesters (once in a gooseberry bush near the Red Spot) waiting for their main food source, the scotch thistle, to mature. Its seeds are much like nyjer seeds, which now attract these birds in large numbers to winter feeders. Feed them and they will come, someone said.

William Butler Yeats mentions goldfinches, or a European version, in his poem "The Lake Isle of Innisfree."

There midnight's all a glimmer, and noon a purple glow,
And evening full of the linnet's wings.

Three other finches that sometimes arrive in great numbers are the royal purple finches, the delicate pine siskins, and the restless redpolls:

Purple Finch

Pine Siskin

Common Redpoll

Every few years the finches *erupt* in huge numbers to exploit a regionally abundant crop of pinecones with their seeds in what's called a mast year. In the years following, the forests are often quiet as these nomads erupt elsewhere across the immense boreal forests (taiga) of North America and Russia.

The coniferous trees "don't wish" their seeds—their children—to be devoured by the seed predators: finches, squirrels, mice, blue jays, and so on. They grip their babies tightly to the cone and shield them with hard scales, but the crossbills have the key to unlock these small black treasures. The finches and the firs are evolving together, like the wolves and the deer. The trees, however, have another and more effective strategy to avoid predators. The nature writer Bernd Heinrich describes this tactic in his insightful book *The Trees in My Forest*:

> One problem with loading up the seeds with a large food store is that it invites predators to eat them. . . . Blue jays and squirrels eat nuts, carrying off and planting the surplus they can't immediately eat. Most other seed predators are not so helpful. To have a surplus of seeds that will not be eaten, the tree generally produces no seeds for a few years—until all of its seed predators have starved or left. Then the tree suddenly puts out a giant crop that hopefully won't be completely devoured.

There is also a strong tendency for different species of trees to synchronize their mast years, so all the food crops fail in the same year. This failure will result in a mass exodus of those that can fly or in an extirpation of those that cannot.

The process by which a single species of bird or mammal adjusts to a new environment, and diversifies into many new species to fill every available ecological niche, is called *adaptive radiation*. Darwin's dull finches and those jewels of great boreal forests are both excellent examples of this evolutionary principle.

The finches fly on through the evergreen forests in their eternal pursuit of the pinecones. And for their part, the pines protect their young from the finches' deadly chase. Each hones the other to perfection by natural selection. It's not only the weak and the old who falter and fall; it's the inefficient—the ones who stray too far from the edge. To those who do the dance, whether pine or finch, belongs the day and the future. It's not a good day to die—it never is. So the finches fly on through the evergreen forests.

The Seed Warriors—Nomads of the Boreal Forest

CHAPTER—9

A GAZE OF RACCOONS

She turned to the sunlight
And shook her yellow head,
And whispered to her neighbor:
"Winter is dead."
A. A. Milne, "When We Were Very Young"

The Ides of March is announced by the male red-winged blackbird's call—a classic spring sound of wetlands across this great continent. Blackbirds arrive quietly in the dead of night by twos and threes. Because their regular haunts of bulrushes and bogs are still frozen and foodless, they fly to the fir trees near my bird feeder. Here they hide until the first gray of morning fills the east and the barred owls cease calling. Then at some unknown signal, they shake themselves, ruffling their feathers and expanding their breasts and tails. Their wings drape like a cloak, exposing large red insignia, fringed with gold, that flash from their shoulders. And like some avian Pavarotti, they burst forth with their irrepressible aria *conk-la-ree, conk-la-ree, conk-la-ree!*

To rivals it asserts, "This land is my land," but to everyone else it declares, "Winter is dead," although the woods are still knee-deep in snow.

Red-Winged Blackbird

Raccoon on the Ides of March

I have placed trail cameras in the forests of the farm for over two decades. Every path, burrow, pond, beaver damn, deer kill, and food cache has been memorialized. Originally, I used a film camera, but I quickly graduated to digital varieties when these became available. Instead of 24 shots on a roll of film, I have had as many as 8,000 on an SD card. To not startle the animal with a flashbulb, the newer cameras use infrared photography at night. Rarely does a bird or mammal realize it is being photographed, so all its behavior is natural. Downloading the SD card onto my computer is like Christmas when you were a child: you never know what you are going to get.

This activity is just a more sophisticated version of what my cousin and I did when our earth was young and the summers green and carefree. But now I search for rare animals such as moose, wolves, or bears, and I am seldom disappointed. You can take the boy out of the land, but you can't take the land out of the boy!

Among the many surprises were photographs of raccoons on the Ides of March year after year—sometimes even earlier. They often walk as if on stilts trying to avoid touching the snow with their dexterous hands and feet. Why are they not in their cozy dens? Raccoons are best classified as winter sleepers like bears, not true hibernators like woodchucks. At that time of year, however, there is absolutely nothing for them to eat. On the other hand, they could be a sandwich for a wolf or an omelet for an eagle. So why are they out?

Well it must be about sex! These are males searching for somnolent females for coitus. If he finds one, it may take him one to two weeks to win her over. Finally they mate for an hour or more after which she immediately falls back to sleep. In disgust, he leaves and returns to his original den and sleeps another month to rise with the bears in the middle of April. And with that one foray, he has completed the entirety of his parental duties—the rest is up to her, so let her sleep.

Most mammals have a penis bone, humans do not; instead we have Viagra®. This bone retracts with the rest of the penis and helps to keep it rigid during coitus. Most penis bones are straight, but the raccoon's curves and hooks into the female's pelvis. It gets the job done! The photograph of this bone does not show its actual size; it's bigger (4 inches or 10 cm long).

About two months after dad's hard work, the kits (cubs) are born totally helpless, blind, and deaf. Now mother's work begins as she nurses them for 16 weeks, teaching them everything she knows. They stay close to her until the next spring when the males, like bear cubs, leave the natal territory to prevent inbreeding. We are their main predators with our guns and automobiles—wolves, owls, and eagles also take a few of the young.

Raccoon
Penis
Bone

When Do We Get a Turn?

Many country boys and girls keep pet raccoons, but these animals make good pets only if they are captured quite young. My cousin and I had a youngster; he was not long out of his den before being leg-trapped in a corn patch. These traps are heartless devices—one of our most cruel inventions.

When a local farmer gave us this young raccoon, incredibly, the trap was still on his right front paw. Immediately we removed it and applied some ointment my aunt provided us, along with a warning not to get bitten. Over time, the paw healed but it was never fully functional although he could climb trees. This youngster learned to trust us; we were his parents. He roamed freely but not too far from the house we built for him. After all, that's where the food was. He ate everything—everything—we collected: kitchen scraps, crayfish, frogs, earthworms, corn, and so on. The crayfish seemed to be his favorite: he always ate them first from a bucket, seemingly washing each as his meal progressed. He gained a lot of weight, and spent the winter in the woodshed, but he visited the barn most days to lap up the milk we put out for the cats as we milked the cows. The cats were not amused, but neither were they eaten! The following spring he wandered off in search of a mate, and we never saw him again. I hope his genes still run over this land and climb these trees.

An adult raccoon, despite its smallness, is a ball of fury when confronted. In protection of their young, mother raccoons are absolutely fearless; by transforming into balls of ferocity, they will drive off adult bears. For their part, bears wisely *do not eat* raccoons; it's not worth their trouble, but raccoons and bears will dine together.

Bear and Raccoons at Supper

Mrs. Marx, a mother raccoon, was out for a little lunch at the Cracked Corn Café with her six madcap sons Chico, Harpo, Groucho, Gummo, Zeppo, and Mannie (*see* the photograph "Bear and Raccoons at Supper"). Unfortunately, a large black bear also went to dine at the same café. The six babies wondered at the size of mom's new boyfriend, but the bear appears totally uninterested in the raccoons who remain guarded with this new friendship. The following day, meeting at the same café with the black swimming pool, events were not so amiable.

In recent years, as well as photographs, I take videos. A few of these are available on my YouTube website. To see the death defying Mrs. Marx, search "Raccoons and Bear in a Scuffle." The whole video is just 47 seconds long, but the real action takes place in the first 16 seconds. I would suggest you watch it a few times to convince yourself that the big "scary" bear was startled when the baby raccoons (the Marx brothers) approached him and acted instinctively, but with no real intent to kill them. Then, seemingly from out of nowhere, mother raccoon charges the bear by running right under his jaw. Unexpectedly, he turns and flees while Mrs. Marx stands her ground victorious, but her boys climb the nearest tree. Five minutes later, they are all eating together as if nothing had happened.

The photograph "Mrs. Marx goes to War" was captured from the above-mentioned video. The larger white circle indicates Mrs. Marx, a fuzzy ball of fury, so much so that the bear has become airborne in fear. The smaller circle shows one of the Marx brothers becoming tree borne for the same reason.

Mrs. Marx Goes to War

The raccoon's teeth reflect its adaptation as an omnivore as do ours. Once upon a time, my cousin and I, while sitting on a large outcropping of the Canadian Shield, found the skull of a raccoon. I still have it. It was lying in the sun, clean and white, resting on a small bed of moss growing in a crack in the granite. I counted the teeth, 20 on the bottom, 20 on top, for a total of 40. We wondered how it came to be there and what its story might be. I slipped the skull inside my shirt, and we took it home, walking barefoot along the cool cow paths.

These 40 teeth come in four varieties: incisors, canines, car-nassials, and molars. This animal could clip, slash, rip, tear, and grind anything, which makes the raccoon a generalist and more likely to be a survivor in changing times. In contrast, the koala, with its eucalyptus-only diet, is a specialist. It's the woodchuck and the fox all over again; this generalist trait may yet allow rac-coons to conquer the world.

Although native to North America, these masked rascals have now invaded mainland Europe. The occasion of their arrival on that continent is bizarre. At least one major cause was Reichsmarschall Hermann Goering, who in 1934 was in charge of Germany's forests. (His qualifications for this position are quite unclear.) Anyhow, Herr Goering released a few of these bandits to be shot for "sport," but the raccoons, of course, had other ideas. And at the time of my writing, they have overcome all of Germany. Unlike the Allied Powers, their occupation will

Ich bin ein Berliner!

be permanent—they will never leave. Count on it! The British press has had fun with these rogues, referring to them as Nazi raccoons. The British, however, had best not chuckle too much, as their turn is next. You can count on that too!

For better or worse, I regularly fed cracked corn to the rac-coons and to whomever else wandered by. Like humans, they don't know when to stop eating so many became obese, very obese. Nothing would disturb them at their dinner, neither rain nor cold nor bears nor myself. Some nights, I would shine my large flashlight on them, but they only looked up in unison *to gaze* in my direction. Occasionally, a few deer or a lone bear would join them, but never a mother bear and her cubs.

There Goes the Diet Again!

The photo "There goes the diet again!" shows raccoons perhaps having their last meal for five frigid months; from November to late April, they must live on their stored fat. This layer of fat and their naturally thick fur act as insulation to keep the heat in, not the cold out. Cold doesn't exist; it's just the absence of heat—bald isn't a hair color; it's just an absence of hair. During the winter, if the temperature rises above freezing, they may venture out of their dens and be fortunate enough to find some carrion. More likely they will become prey to wolves and possibly fishers. As winter in Ontario is a time of starvation, raccoons gorge themselves in the fall. For these rascals it is not survival of the fittest but survival of the fattest.

Raccoons are nocturnal and not as abundant in the country as in the city—you could wander in the woods for days and never see one. So imagine my surprise when they arrived at the Cracked Corn Café in gangs. This cascade of raccoons was reminiscent of some lines from Lewis Carroll's famous nonsense poem *The Walrus and the Carpenter*, "And thick and fast they came at last, / And more, and more, and more–."

Some nights there were 18 or more. I wouldn't have believed there were that many on both farms. Like the bumblebees, they never fought with each other, although occasionally one would cry out a warning to another over some unknown infraction of "raccoon law." Mostly they huddled together like sheep and were almost as large. By size alone, however, I could no longer distinguish between adults and last spring's kits. Childhood was receding for the Marx brothers.

What a Great Restaurant!

The spring field was the only one my uncle could plow other than the vegetable gardens near the house. The others were ground where only Sisyphus might have worked moving stones and breaking plows. Over the actual spring was a small wooden shed to prevent leaves and other debris from falling into the water, which bubbled up mysteriously through the sandy bottom. The adults said this bottom was quicksand, but it seemed firm enough when we poked it with a long stick.

This field was cultivated manually with a horse and an ages-old plow, as if we were in ancient Egypt. And as my uncle plowed, we heedless youths followed to see what wonders might be uncovered. We each had a Crown preserving jar retrieved from my aunt's pantry and surely without her permission. These jars were to collect the treasures from the freshly furrowed field. Chief among these was the incredible star-nosed mole.

Star-nosed Mole: Essence of Ugliness

Both my cousin and I viewed this unlikely creature as the essence of ugliness—our attitude like Darwin's toward the marine iguanas of the Galapagos, whom he calls the "imps of darkness." The mole's nose had 22 protuberances (we loved to count) like freshly extruded hamburger out of a meat grinder and claws so long and sharp they were more suited to tear the furrows of the fields of hell than this pleasant pasture we called the spring field. You might guess we killed something that ugly, but, strangely, we let it go.

Young Raccoon: Essence of Cuteness

Beauty truly is in the eye of the beholder: we see the star-nosed mole as butt ugly yet the baby raccoon as adorable. But why? Some readers may think my question is frivolous because the mole with its digging claws seems a creature from the movie *Dawn of the Dead* while the raccoon looks just arrived fresh from the nursery. Star-nosed moles, however, must see (yes, they have beady little eyes) each other as the heart of hotness or the entire species would disappear in a single generation. I repeat, beauty is in the eye of the beholder. The question remains, "Why do *we see* one as ugly and the other as attractive?" The whole cosmetic industry rests on the answer.

To us the cutest infant in all creation is the human infant. In its presence, we get all mushy and gooey inventing a vocabulary of oohs and aahs. We are attracted by the baby's large head and eyes, high cranium, short legs and arms, button nose, and, of course, its perfect unblemished symmetry. This baby is our gold standard for cuteness. So naturally animals having the characteristics of human infants attract us most strongly.

And this cuteness has a high survival value. Our ancestors who originally found these characteristics appealing would clearly leave more offspring than those who did not. If natural selection favors a physical attribute, you will soon see more of it. For example, in the artificial selection of dogs (aka selective breeding), *we select* for cute, fluffy, adorable. For vegetables, *we select* for sweetness, size, and texture. In both cases, we end up with what we want. Maltese terriers and diminutive Chihuahuas wouldn't last overnight in the forest but they thrive on your bed. And those huge, sweet strawberries you purchase in the supermarket never grew in nature's wild fields. Chipmunks pick the wild varieties fitting several into their small mouths and cheeks at one time to carry back to their larders.

Consider the star-nosed mole and the raccoon baby pictured above. You can't even see the mole's eyes or its face because of the branching ornate nose. On the other hand, the baby raccoon has a large head, prominent eyes overarched with fur suggestive of eyebrows, short front legs reminiscent of arms, a button nose, and perfect symmetry. And the black mask—like women's eyeliner—is universally attractive to humans. All this regularity of feature is set in a field of soft-looking fur.

The evolutionary biologist Steven Jay Gould in one of his famous essays "A Biological Homage to Mickey Mouse" (free online) points out that even cartoon characters can evolve. Consider the images of Mickey taken from Gould's essay. The one on the left is from the first movie *Steamboat Willie* (1928) revealing a somewhat obnoxious rodent. This figure evolved to the juvenile Mickey on the right: bigger eyes, bigger head, large cranial vault, shorter arms, and incidentally much better behaved. Here we have the Mickey of today's Disney world enterprises—a well-behaved, cute, childlike creation. This evolution was viewer driven—Gould speculates that perhaps even the artists were unaware of this progression.

Evolution of Mickey Mouse © Walt Disney Productions

Charles Darwin noted that our tastes may be no less evolved than our brains and our bodies. And what is true of humans is equally true of the entire panorama of life. When there is a separation between us and another mammal, the difference is always a matter of degree not of kind.

Surprisingly, there is a side of us that cannot help looking at road accidents, deformities, and star-nosed moles. When my cousin and I found the decomposing carcass of the bear crawling with a million maggots, we were transfixed with revulsion but took home a tooth to commemorate the event. Who hasn't slowed down on a freeway to view some carnage or other, and the "news" is usually bad by definition.

In the natural world, as well, there is always room for death by accident, disease, predation, or privation. Without death, there would be no life. In late June, a mother raccoon and her four rambunctious kits came regularly to my Cracked Corn Café.

The Three Stooges plus Shemp

Now raccoon kits are always mischievous; it's part of their personality, part of growing up. But these four were particularly obnoxious, always tumbling, pushing, running, climbing. So much so that I named them after the Three Stooges, a slapstick American vaudeville and comedy act. Slowly it became apparent to me that their mother was missing. Where was she? The likelihood of her abandoning her babies, however annoying they might be, was virtually nil. Yet, I never saw her again.

Are You My Mummy?

But the cubs still came every night and, before long, during the day. They were always together. I expanded the menu at the café to include some kibble and canned dog food, which my patrons seemed to enjoy. Their daily presence did, however, give me the opportunity to photograph one of nature's most endearing characters.

We're Hanging in There!

If these young raccoons hadn't been regular and valued customers at the Cracked Corn Café, it's likely they would have perished. Sometimes, another mother of the same species adopts orphaned babies, and, more often than you might expect, we find cross-species adoptions and friendships. Our mythology is alive with such stories, going back to Rome's founders Romulus and Remus and beyond. Humans keep pets of various species, so we should expect non-human animals to have friends from other species,* and they do.

The Stooges, All Tuckered Out

These four bandits spent the summer and the fall dining at the café, but I couldn't discover their denning tree. In November the first snow fell, and then it was quite easy to follow their little handprints back to their hotel. The two farms are separated by a fence of fieldstones interspersed with ancient maple trees—old even when my mother as a child danced through these fields. Over time, black carpenter ants found their way into the trees' interior and constructed galleries of nests. In turn, crow-sized pileated woodpeckers attacked these ants creating oval excavations. And depending on the size of the ant infestation, some of these holes were large enough that a human might spend the night in one. Now my four rascals never wandered far from the

---

* For examples, search "cross-species friendships" and "cross-species adoptions" on the Internet.

Pileated Woodpecker

Cracked Corn Café, so their residence in one of these patriarchal maples with a convenient bird-built apartment was not surprising. They spent the winter there sleeping together as they might have with their mother had she still been alive. Their winter den was visible from my home by the Red Spot.

The first time I saw them the following spring, they were still together. Although I have referred to these raccoons as males, I didn't know their true gender until they had overwintered. Shortly after that springtime visit, I saw only two raccoons—females, I now believe, because males like young bears leave their birth area to prevent incest, sometimes traveling great distances. All four were survivors with a little help from a friend. They had escaped predation from wolves, eagles, possibly fishers, and the ravages of disease, particularly distemper. In my ramblings, both with my cousin and alone, I have come upon several dead baby raccoons, and I always assumed they had died from distemper, a common killer of this species.

What I deduced were the two females continued to visit the café and eventually they brought their kits. As they knew each other, there were few negative exchanges and no major infractions of raccoon law. But the males had harder courses with unknown outcomes. Childhood with all its antics and lack of responsibility was behind them, never to return. Now they were adults and had to stand and deliver, to face life's challenges. It's a darker world, with fewer options—a world we must war against to hold on to youth's optimism. All of us should heed Dylan Thomas's advice, "Do not go gentle into that good night."

CHAPTER—10

WALKER'S POND

I come from haunts of coot and hern;
I make a sudden sally
And sparkle out among the fern,
To bicker down a valley.
Tennyson, "The Brook"

Whack goes the beaver's tail scattering the birds from the trees and the bushes. The spring peepers cease their incessant song; a once sleepy muskrat plops below the pond's dark glassy surface. And the painted turtles sunning themselves on a floating log slip silently into their watery realm. A few birds hold their ground crouching low on their nests while the bittern disappears into the bulrushes. By now, the beaver has already reached the lodge to be greeted by her two kits.

The cause of this disruption in the daily life of the pond is a canoe carrying two people, a man and a woman. Since it's spring and the beavers have babies, the young woman *pleads* with the man not to trap. But he says they need the money the fur will bring, so the trap is set by the lodge's underwater entrance. They paddle away without speaking, and the pond returns to its timeless ways.

Beaver Lodge on Walker's Pond

The following morning the two canoeists return to discover both the trap and the beaver missing. The man knew he had securely staked the trap to the pond bottom placing it at the underwater entry to the lodge. Yet in her desperation, the mother beaver had pulled the stake out of the mud and died an agonizing death elsewhere, the trap's steel jaws clamping inexorably on her soft body while water flooded her lungs.

The trapper is disgusted at this outcome because not only had he lost the beaver fur but also the beaver had lost its life, and all for nothing—nothing at all. He unsuccessfully drags the pond for her body. And, as a last resort, he destroys the dam partly draining the pond, but to no avail. All the life of this pond will now die; the dam buster has become the destroyer of worlds.

The Beaver—Creator of New Worlds

The trapper was an Englishman, Archie Belaney (aka Grey Owl), and the woman was a Mohawk, Gertrude Bernard (aka Anahareo), and their story was only beginning. But I'll let Grey Owl speak for himself from his book *Pilgrims of the Wild* in which he recounts this scene and its astonishing sequel:

So we turned to go, finally and for good. As we were leaving I heard behind me a light splash, and looking back saw what appeared to be a muskrat lying on top of the water along side of the house. Determined to make this wasted day pay, I threw up my gun, and standing up in the canoe to get a better aim, prepared to shoot. At that distance a man could never miss, and my finger was about to press the trigger when the creature gave a low cry, and at the same instant I saw, right in my line of fire another, who gave out the same peculiar call. They could both be gotten with the one charge of shot.

Anahareo with a Kit

They gave voice again, and this time the sound was unmistakeable—they were young beaver! I lowered my gun and said:

"There are your kittens."

The instinct of a woman spoke out at once.

"Let us save them," cried Anahareo excitedly, and then in a lower voice, "It is up to us, after what we've done."

And truly what had been done here looked now to be an act of brutal savagery. And with some confused thought of giving back what I had taken, some dim idea of atonement, I answered,

"Yes; we have to. Let's take them home." It seemed the only fitting thing to do.

For the beaver and the two people in the canoe, that was the day everything changed. Anahareo encouraged Grey Owl to write books and articles on conservation, and with the help of their two pet beavers, they became worldwide celebrities. Fame followed! David and Richard Attenborough attended one of Grey Owl's conservation talks in England and were greatly impressed. Much later Richard directed the film *Grey Owl* starring Pierce Brosnan. Belaney sat for a portrait by Yousef Karsh (reproduced here), met the king, and was feted everywhere.

After he died suddenly at 49 of pneumonia, his double life was revealed, but, in retrospect, none of that mattered a damn. What remains of his life is monumental, as if a sculptor had blown away the chips from his marble or the nonsense from his existence to reveal its core. What remains is the restoration of the beaver that faced extinction when he and Anahareo picked up their cause and

Grey Owl

their babies. Not only were the beaver restored but also their dams and the incredible variety of life that the beaver encouraged all over this land.

In those youthful days, my cousin and I never saw a beaver nor walked across a beaver dam. Walden Pond was a cranberry bog, and Walker's Pond a marsh, and all the others mere puddles in the springtime. So neither these places nor their names existed.

When we were young boys, everything was new and we were fond of naming places and things. There was *snake rock*, a place where you could always find several cast-off snakeskins. The *bluebird fence post*—always with a nest. The *pony tree*—so deformed its trunk was horizontal, creating a place to pretend to ride. The *snow apple tree*—always in my memory laden with apples. The *fallow field*—a narrow opening in the forest. The *back-barn flat*—the most easterly part of the farm and now part of mine.

But we never named the ponds for there were none to name. Now that my cousin is gone, I take it as my obligation to name these places. And it is Walker's Pond, named for two sisters, his mother and mine, that I wish to explore. I sincerely thank Grey Owl and Anahareo—the names they preferred—for the return of the beaver and the existence of these ponds with all their phenomenal beauty.

Hooded Mergansers on Walker's Pond: aka Hoodies

Male and Female Belted Kingfishers

Today, Walker's Pond is a haven for birds: mergansers, wood ducks, herons, and kingfishers. The rattling call of the belted kingfisher, once heard, is never forgotten. Although they breed all across North America to the tree line, they are not a common bird. They fascinated my cousin and me, so much so that we were determined to find their nest. Ponds are their favorite hunting places, especially in springtime when the water is relatively clear, allowing for easy viewing of the minnows, but rivers and brooks will do. We had no idea where they nested—trees, bushes, barns, on the ground . . . . Who knew? One day while catching minnows in Walker's Brook, we heard their distinctive call and saw one fly from a hole in the sandbank of this stream. We thought its nest must be at the end of that tunnel.

The reader might ask why we wished to find their nest. The nasty truth is we were nasty boys with a small collection of bird's eggs

Cowbird Egg in an
Eastern Phoebe's Nest

Eastern Bluebird Eggs

and nests. The cobalt blue of the bluebird's egg was a favorite. The tiny sprinkled-in-paprika eggs of the chickadee were highly prized. If we already had a particular set of eggs, we didn't collect another; however, we often removed the egg of the brood parasitic brown-headed cowbird (*see* photograph)—so we did some good. Starling, barn swallow, and robin eggs all graced our collection, and, for reasons I will never comprehend, his mother and mine let us store these eggs and nests in the china cabinet. Now mind you we had no china, but obviously our mothers hoped to. This arrangement was unhygienic, but the cabinet was a beautiful display case and most astonishing to visitors.

Back to the kingfisher nest. We walked home (some distance) to collect a shovel and a small pickaxe from the woodshed and returned to do the excavating. As I recall, we were surprised at how long we had to dig because of the burrow's depth. After what seemed hours, we reached the nest only to be disappointed. Oh, we found the eggs, but they were all chicken-egg white—no beautiful markings whatsoever.

My cousin, who was always thinking about these things, said that because the eggs were in the dark—not even the kingfishers saw them—markings weren't needed. "Needed for what?" I asked. All the other eggs with streaks, splashes, and spots needed these for camouflage, but the eggs of birds that nested in cavities and burrows didn't. That day we almost became biologists—I will never forget his insight. Darwin would have been proud of us.

Male Kingfisher (left) at Nest Hole

As eggs that are hidden in cavities or the soil (turtles) have no need of camouflage, they're chalk white. Additionally, because there's no danger of falling from cliffs or open nests, they're spherical. At first glance, the sphere's shining white surface is mildly interesting, but your attention promptly shifts to the other's intriguing lacework patterns. Plainness makes us sleepy; patterns captivate. That's why we two young nest robbers were disappointed with our heist.

Patterned

Plain

Kingfisher Egg   Grouse Egg

Both my cousin and I knew the male and female kingfishers were colored differently, but we didn't know which was which. We had no bird guide. Indeed, we had no books, except an old family bible on a lectern at the top of the stairs beside a stuffed great horned owl. Since the adults never talked about birds other than farm fowl, we didn't ask them.

Now that I'm older, I know the belted kingfisher is one of the very few species in which the female is more brightly colored than the male (*see* photograph). The male has a single blue band across his white breast while the female, a blue and a chestnut band. When I discovered this, I thought of an extension to my cousin's distant insight. Because no predator can see the brightly colored female in the blackness of her burrow, she could be attired in Joseph's coat of many colors and it wouldn't matter.

Previously I mentioned that we'll explore Walker's Pond, which was created by the dam on the brook. Specifically, we'll explore it on one morning, 23 April, Shakespeare's birthday.

Most of the photographs in this chapter were taken that morning including the picture of the kingfishers that were catching and swallowing stickleback minnows head first, the same sort of fish my cousin and I often caught.

Stickleback Minnow

Beavers are what biologists call a keystone species—without them entire ecosystems would cease to exist. On the morning of 23 April, only part of their pond was ice free; most lakes, streams, and ponds were still frozen over. This effect concentrated the wildlife to those few areas with open water. The beaver below was a full-fledged member of the lodge shown on the initial page of this chapter, and this morning may have been his first time in the sunlight since the freeze up last fall.

Beaver at Breakfast on Walker's Pond

Canada Goose Nest

The photo of the beaver's home shows a hidden treasure the reader may have overlooked, so I've reproduced that picture here. On the left side is a Canada goose incubating her clutch of eggs. She did this every year and without protest from the lodge's builders. It was a good place for a nest, safe from most land predators. Geese, however, are not helpless but rather vigorous defenders of their nest and territory—a foolish fox that approaches a nest is certain to receive a beating. Geese have two nasty weapons: the bite from their beak and the bruising from their wings.

Canada Geese: The Northern Express

A long, long time ago, before I was cast out of paradise into the city, my cousin and I would watch the spring and fall migrations of the invincible Canada goose. Once while near, perhaps even on, the Red Spot overlooking our valley, we counted 42 enormous flocks on a single day northward bound for Hudson Bay.

They formed undulating skeins in their classic "V" formations with the largest gander generally in the lead. They chattered, honked, and squawked the whole time. I thought they were encouraging each other, saying,

"We can do this."

"Hang in there."

"Just another thousand miles to Hudson Bay."

As we looked out over the land and the sky, something robust and primal rose within us and, although speechless, we knew we were witness to a powerful ritual. I can still touch that feeling as their voices echo in my head—this was our place and our valley was green indeed.

Even the domesticate geese in our barnyard were not to be trifled with; they had huge sturdy wings and a neck the size of a man's forearm. Our bare legs marked with bites and bruises were witness to their beaks and wings. If we saw any of these free-range bullies, my cousin and I would race across the barnyard and into the forest. After one particularly bad encounter, we each collected a long stick and thumped them a few times on that part of their body opposite the head.

One goose egg will fill a frying pan, and it has the same taste and texture as a chicken's egg. Plus the goose grease was pure white and excellent for hands and boots, or so our grandfather said. Perhaps that's why he kept them. But the meat was distasteful and incredibly fatty; dining on goose was like eating a ball of suet. Worst of all, we were forever stepping in their poop and having it squish up between our bare toes.

Male Wood Ducks: aka Woodies

Also on the pond that morning were wood ducks. If someone were to ask you to name the most beautiful bird in North America, the male wood duck (pictured here) would be an excellent answer. Like hooded mergansers, they nest in woodpecker holes or other tree cavities, and because of this, they have taken readily to the nest boxes I've placed on dead pond trees (snags) in the winter. Both wood ducks and hooded mergansers (woodies and hoodies) will lay eggs in the same nest box to be incubated by the one laying the most eggs. When the eggs hatch these fluffy babies must leap from great heights to a pond's surface or a forest's floor. Surprisingly they are rarely injured.

As boys, we never saw one of these ducks. As I mentioned, we had no books, magazines, or newspapers, though we had a small colored calendar with a picture of a wood duck for April— a tiny treasure. The colors seemed so unreal that I dreamed of finding one, and now I have. Nature can be extravagant! And remember all their astounding color is to impress the female. We primates are just passing observers to this parade of splendor. The female, on the other hand, wears only a little white eye shadow, but he's impressed.

Wood Ducks in Love

Male hooded mergansers are no less splendid although as boys we were entirely ignorant of their existence. The females have a drab body, but again their mates seemed greatly impressed. Perhaps it's the hair (*see* the photos)!

Female   Male

"Hooded Mergansers in Winter" is a painting by the renowned wildlife artist Robert Bateman. He describes "hoodies" as follows:

> In many ways, the hooded merganser is one of the most elegant of waterfowl. The striking black, white and vermiculated rust gives it an almost exotic look. The silky crest and golden eyes increase the effect . . . .

The Happy Couple

Smiling Female Mallard with Eggs and Husband

At the north end of the pond furthest from the dam, I chanced upon a mallard duck already incubating her eggs with her drake ostensibly on guard—a scene of perfect domesticity.

There are those, and they are many, who see little or no value in nature and certainly none in swamps and marshes. These people live for what we see in the film *Manufactured Landscapes*[*]: colossal factories, mega-quarries, and mammoth recycling centers.

Henry David Thoreau was the patron saint of all swamps because he relished being in and writing about them, as these excerpts from his *Journal* reveal:

[M]y temple is the swamp. *Journal,* January 4, 1853

I seemed to have reached a new world, so wild a place...far away from human society. What's the need of visiting far-off mountains and bogs, if a half-hour's walk will carry me into such wildness and novelty? *Journal*, August 30, 1856.

---

[*] *Manufactured Landscapes* is a 2006 documentary film about the work of photographer Edward Burtynsky. Free online.

The Antithesis of a Manufactured Landscape

Everyone in our county made a living by logging or trapping—any farming was strictly subsistence. When I was at the lumber mill, my father did both and more; he was something of a hustler. Behind the kitchen door, hanging from a wooden peg, you could always find a half dozen or more red squirrel skins stretched beyond what seemed possible. My father sold these to buyers who resold them to furriers to be made into coat linings and gloves. He received 50 cents a pelt if the squirrel were shot through the head by a .22 rifle. Many of the men at the mill were paid only $5.00 a month plus room and board, so there was relatively big money in fur, even if it were only squirrel.

From this, you can infer that a mink pelt was worth a fortune. Because there were no beaver ponds, we rarely if ever saw a mink, but we did have an ancient glacial lake, the same lake where Mother Courage had her natal den decades later. This lake took up over half of my grandfather's original farm, and like all such lakes of the Canadian Shield it was filling in; the result was a great surrounding marsh with a floating bog. It was a place of some mystery. The adults told us terrifying and fabulous tales about it: quicksand, no bottom, strange creatures. We were never to go there!

Mystery Lake

There is a safe way, however, to enter this lake from a stream that flows out of it under a road. (The farms are bounded on the east and west sides by parallel roads.) Someone I didn't know must have boated into the lake from the road, and gone fishing; he caught three huge, primitive fish called bowfins. My aunt refused to clean and cook these "fish" because of their snake-like appearance, but my cousin and I were fascinated. The angler also mentioned he had seen a mink in the surrounding marsh. On hearing his news, we were determined to find this fabled mammal.

Mink at Walker's Pond

Mysterious Lake

As we had no boat or canoe, we needed another plan. So the following day we walked up the road to view the lake. On the far side, we could see some high rocks that overlooked a large part of the marsh (*see* satellite view). This would be our destination. First we walked to the old barn, turned west, and marched until we reached the marsh. Turning to our right, and keeping the edge of the marsh in sight, we trekked for a long time before reaching those rocky cliffs—the furthest we had ever been from home. But we had already scared up several partridge, seen three snakes, and found a hawk's nest. So what could go wrong?

When we arrived at this outcropping of the Canadian Shield, we lay down and surveyed the marsh. Because we were poor—this was a later revelation—we had no camera or binoculars, just the sharp vision of youth. Normally we were impatient wigglers and squirmers, but not today. We were on a quest! An hour must have passed and maybe another before my cousin saw the mink.

Incredible Flying Mink

It was a beautiful creature, running this way and that, appearing and disappearing at will. We were totally engrossed as we watched its every move. Twice it disappeared below the water's black surface only to emerge in a few minutes. Here was a creature wondrously adapted to an environment we found hostile and dangerous. Such are marvels of time and tiny changes.

As I recall, my cousin was proud of seeing the mink first, and he playfully punched my arm to show this. Because I was older, perhaps he thought I would find it before him. After a time the mink vanished, and we left for home. Together we decided to tell no one fearing some adult would trap it for its valuable fur, not to mention that disclosure would reveal our journey to the forbidden lake. Arriving home about suppertime, we let my aunt tend to our numerous blackfly and mosquito bites for the blood was running down our faces. She naively asked where we had been, and we babbled something about walking far up the road, which was the truth, but not the full truth. This deception troubled us, but the insect bites gave us no concern because we had found the mink at the mysterious lake.

Going on these adventures is part of growing up, trusting yourself, and testing your limits. And although neither of us was yet ten years old, we had done this. Our quest was a success!

Beaver dams, unlike most human concrete barriers, allow water to pass through. These furry creators desire to maintain the water at a fixed height to protect their lodge not submerge it. So every beaver dam has an outlet forming a rivulet or small stream.

Cranes over the Shield

Walker's Pond begins at the outlet of a high beaver dam on the Fifty Acre Pond (*see* map), a stop-off point for the spectacular sandhill crane with its haunting, rattling call. To "sing" as they fly, cranes keep their necks straight out, unlike the herons that glide sedately with theirs folded back in an "S" position.

Haunt of the Great Blue Heron

The brook murmurs on through the hardwood forest where deer, moose, wolf, raccoon, fox, and a hundred other creatures pause to drink. It arrives at the marshy end of Long Pond and takes its time reaching the far end. At the face of the second dam, smallmouth bass school and pumpkinseed sunfish and myriads of minnows reside in a place where otters come to feed.

A decade ago, long after my cousin left us, I was exploring an area near Long Pond with a friend. It was late April, and mercifully, the blackflies and mosquitoes were not yet active. The day was still and pleasant as we walked north into unfamiliar territory. Then we heard the sound of wind. This seemed odd because everything near us was deadly calm. As we continued to walk, the sound grew louder and louder, and so did our curiosity.

We reached the south end of Long Pond where Walker's Brook enters, and by then the noise was impressive, if not intimidating. We continued in the direction of the "wind" each too proud to tell the other how he really felt! As we approached the far end with the dam, the uproar was overpowering.

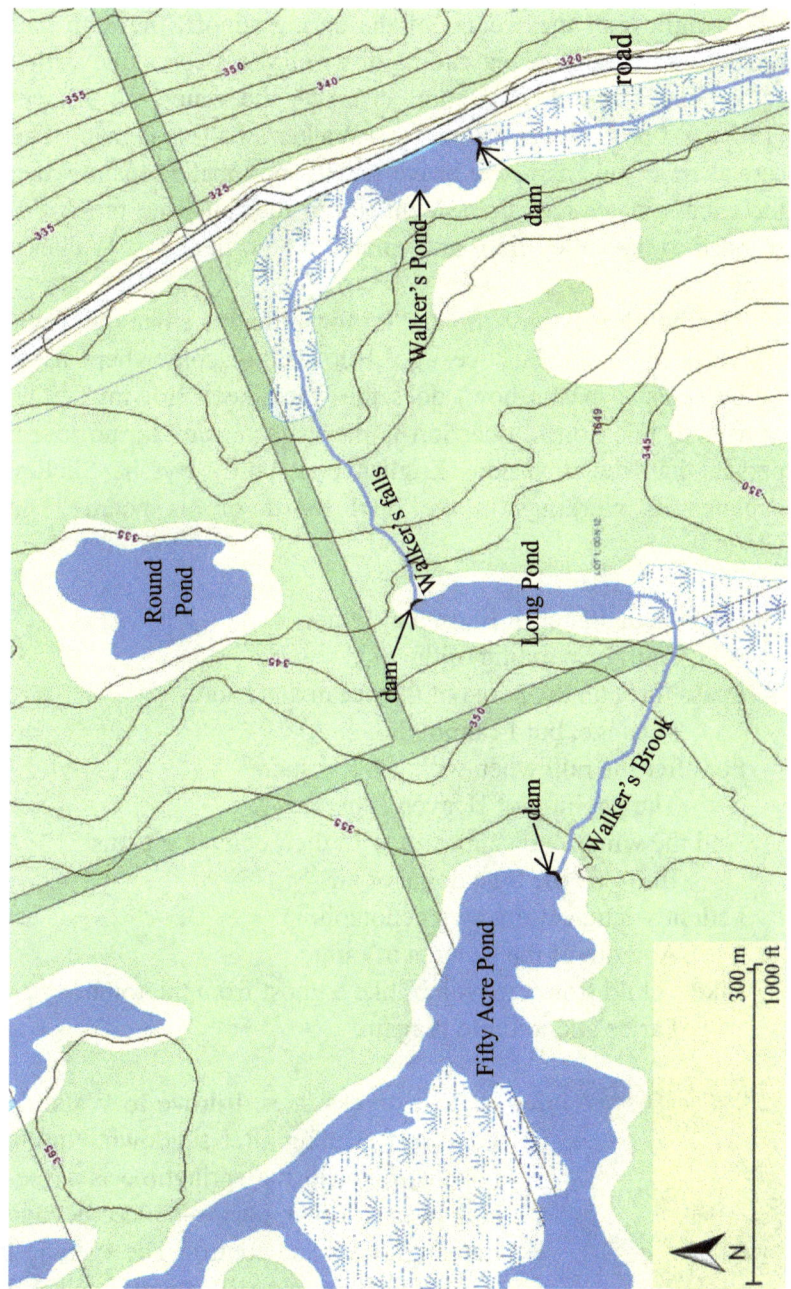

The Watershed for Walker's Pond

At the same instant, we both recognized the source of the whirlwind. With the weight of the spring runoff, the dam had broken and water was cascading down into a steep stone valley at breakneck speed. In a short distance, the water fell 50 feet (15.2 m). I promptly christened this Walker's Falls (*see* map). The caretakers of this dam, the beavers, will soon make repairs when the excess water has drained out. From the falls, the brook descended to the valley floor and entered the north end of Walker's Pond.

This brook may have floated on for millennia since the glaciers receded in the last ice age. But a child somewhere asks, "Why (he/she means how) does the water keep flowing?" The answer to this honest question is the *water cycle* and no less a person than the illustrious English poet Percy Bysshe Shelley explains its workings in the final stanza of his poem "The Cloud":

I am the daughter of Earth and Water,
    And the nursling of the Sky;
I pass through the pores of the ocean and shores;
    I change, but I cannot die.
For after the rain when with never a stain
    The pavilion of Heaven is bare,
And the winds and sunbeams with their convex gleams
    Build up the blue dome of air,
I silently laugh at my own cenotaph,
    And out of the caverns of rain,
Like a child from the womb, like a ghost from the tomb,
    I arise and unbuild it again.

Spring Peeper

Two weeks later, I drove to Walker's Pond one evening after sundown. Now a pond at night in the springtime is a special, even spiritual, place—a place beyond human powers and control. The evening I arrived at the pond still seems fresh and new. The spring peepers are in full chorus, creating the loudest sound for their size of any living creature. Only the male peepers sing; the females judge their performance. These tiny frogs—they can sit on your thumb—are easy to identify by the faint cross on their back (*see* photo), yet they are incredibly elusive.

Beavers, forever at work it seems, cause ripples on the black surface of the pond and the moon shivers. I can hear whip-poor-wills call in the distance as a night squadron of Canada geese honk their goodbyes northward bound for the tundra. Something splashes at the water's edge, perhaps a deer or bear taking an evening drink. Others join the peeper chorale: western chorus and wood frogs. A barred owl shouts out his curious call and two wolves howl at the slowly rising moon.

As this empowering oratorio of sound rolls over me, I stand transfixed. It lifts me up; my spirit soars, and I know I can do anything—anything at all. Just as I realize this, the beavers stop swimming. The luminous body of water opens, dark and tranquil, from whose floor the new-bathed stars emerge, and shine upon Eden's pond[*].

---

[*] My thanks to Matthew Arnold's poem *Sohrab and Rustum*.

CHAPTER—11

THE YOUNG PYTHAGOREANS

Now as I was young and easy under the apple boughs
About the lilting house and happy as the grass was green,
The night above the dingle starry,
Time let me hail and climb
Golden in the heydays of his eyes. . .
Dylan Thomas, "Fern Hill"

The open fields were our special domain—the home of bumblebees and wildflowers. Less commonly my cousin and I would see butterflies, meadow voles, woodchucks, innumerable birds, and soaring hawks—all of which the adults called "chicken hawks"—and sometimes, while we ambled through the high wisteria bushes, a bolting deer. And if the partridge were at the height of their population cycle, they were as chickens running through the fields. On rare occasions, we found a dead mouse with kangaroo back legs and a long tail; they were not the mice that ran all through our home. Later I learned these were woodland jumping mice, rarely seen and seldom photographed.

Woodland Jumping Mouse

Every day spent in aimless ambling was certain to reveal some treasure. These were not days subtracted from our young lives but rather extra days, a gift on life's journey.

Flowers were our particular fascination; perhaps it was innate for our grandmother was a master cultivator of domestic varieties. When you don't have technology you can at least have beauty, as our species has had since the great cave paintings at Lascaux and Altamira. Our grandmother knew a thing or two about beauty. As well as cultivate flowers, she would recite or sing Scottish poetry and songs. "Wild Mountain Thyme" was my favorite, and I was particularly fond of the phrase from the chorus "And we'll all go together." But we didn't you know. . . .

> *And we'll all go together*
> *To pluck wild mountain thyme*
> *All around the blooming heather,*
> *Will you go, lassie, go?*

On the original farm where our grandmother held sway, she had a deep red peony bush in her garden. In the spring, ants covered the buds lapping up its nectar. Incredibly, this perennial still blooms every year with a dozen blossoms each the size of a baseball. I can't definitely age this unattended, unfertilized, and almost unseen plant but it is at least a centenarian. There were bleeding hearts, monkshood delphiniums, and lilies that are now, alas, all gone. And although the house has long since burned down, this hardy peony plant still thrives.

Unlike our grandmother, we concentrated on wild varieties of flowers. We were young Pythagoreans for we loved to count. Oh, not as lovesick adolescents might with "she loves me, she loves me not" but just a straightforward enumeration of the flower's petals. At that time, what we found was consistency, and years later we recognized this as a pattern. Let's begin at the beginning. The consistency lay in each *healthy* variety of flower always having a certain number of petals, even if the number were exceedingly large. As we shall see, this regularity also applies to leaves, branches, and seed spirals. Consider the examples pictured here of flowers picked from the field of boyhood dreams:

Trillium: 3 Petals

Saint-John's Wort: 5 Petals

Bloodroot: 8 Petals

Black-Eyed Susan: 13 Petals

Devil's Paintbrush: 21 Petals

Oxeye Daisy: 34 Petals

Sunflower: 55 Petals

Daisy Fleabane: 89 Petals

Every summer evening when we had tired the sun with exploring and sent him down the sky, we would wander out in search of the turkeys or cows, rarely both. These warm, placid creatures had to be sheltered in the safety of our barn. Since the farm was heavily forested, they were usually hard to find, even with the help of our faithful dog Pal. So we would call to them in a smooth comforting voice, "Cooo-bos, cooo-bos, cooo-bos." Typically, they would give themselves away with deep lowing sounds. Well it just so happens that *bos* or $\beta o \varsigma$ is the ancient Greek word for cow. This word had come down through the centuries—to two young boys chasing cattle in the hinterland of Ontario—totally unchanged from the original Greek. That's the wonderful consistency of a word through time and over space. But in the shadowy fields all around us was a design by nature that had endured millions upon millions of years and on every continent. And this is the pattern I wish to investigate.

Years passed and the dreams faded to the back of my mind to make way for more pressing and immediate matters, but they never left me. I suspect we all have such special thoughts, sacred in our memory. One afternoon all that changed! In my mathematics class, the teacher wrote the following sequence of numbers on the blackboard and asked if anyone could discover the next term:

$$1, \ 1, \ 2, \ 3, \ 5, \ 8, \ 13, \ 21, \ 34, \ 55, \ . \ . \ .$$

Without raising my hand or a moment's hesitation, I blurted out "It's 89." These were the numbers my cousin and I had found a decade earlier. I wish he had been with me that day in class, but he quit school early for reasons I never understood.

The teacher was more amazed than annoyed by my outburst; he asked how I knew the answer so quickly. I told him a much-shortened version because one is protective of such precious memories. It was now his turn to amaze me, for the numbers we had stumbled upon as boys were none other than part of the famous Fibonacci sequence named for a medieval mathematician. And the secret for finding the next term in his sequence—as boys we had overlooked this—is marvelously simple: add the preceding two terms to get the next.

For example, 3 + 5 = 8, 21 + 34 = 55, and so on.

As my teacher gave instance after instance of this sequence occuring in nature, my surprise grew—a feeling that lives with me to the present moment.

With composite flowers, meaning those with multiple florets on their heads, you can, by concentrating on the spirals, distinguish a *double Fibonacci pattern*. The head of the oxeye daisy (*see* photo) has 21 spirals going clockwise and 34 going the other way. Hence, at the edge you have 21+34 or 55 special florets we call petals. The 34 spirals are more easily seen near the edge of the head, the 21 nearer the center. Count them! Depending on the size of the particular seed head, composite flowers have different numbers of spirals; nevertheless, they're always neighboring pairs from the Fibonacci sequence.

Oxeye Daisy: 21 Clockwise and 34 Counterclockwise

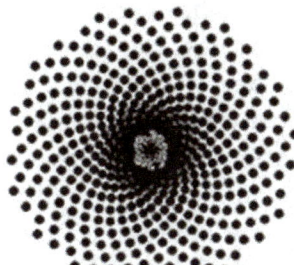

21 clockwise
and
34 counterclockwise
from
500 buds

Sunflower Spirals: 34 Clockwise and 55 Counterclockwise

The pairs commonly found on sunflowers are 21/34, 34/55, 55/89, and, occasionally on a giant, 89/144. These spiral patterns can also be seen on the heads of other composite flowers.

Pineapple

The pineapple, that standard of the modern summer kitchen, has 8 rows of scales sloping to the right, and 13 sloping to the left. With it, and many other fruits and plants, the florets arrange themselves in spirals up the stem. Smaller pineapples can have 5 spirals one way and 8 the other—always these are adjacent Fibonacci pairs. As with sunflowers, this difference is not the result of genetic variation but rather a matter of soil and sunshine.

Besides sunflowers, daisies, and pineapples, nature's best example of the Fibonacci pattern is the pinecone. These range in size from the width of your fingernail to the length of your forearm. The seed warriors chase the kernels of these cones all around the top of the world. In the figure reproduced here, we have a cone on the left with its spirals outlined on the right: 8 solid black or white counterclockwise and 13 banded black and white clockwise. Larger or smaller cones can have different pairs of numbers, but they're consistently adjacent terms from the Fibonacci sequence.

Pine Cone   Pine Cone Spirals

Some readers will point out that I haven't shown examples of flowers with 1 or 2 petals or leaves, the initial terms in the Fibonacci sequence. So consider the jack-in-the-pulpit with 1 leaf that was found by my cousin and me in rare places on our farms. We carried a plant home to ask our grandmother what it was.

Jack-in-the-Pulpit   Dutchman's-Breeches

Besides knowing a thing or two about beauty, she had a wide knowledge of forest plants; some of this was for "medicinal" purposes. At first, she was alarmed and asked if we had eaten any part of this plant. She must have known we were forest grazers so we set her mind at ease; apparently, jack-in-the-pulpit is poisonous. Today we would also label it transgender because most years it alternates from male to female.

Beside the photograph of jack-in-the-pulpit is one of the delicate perennial Dutchman's-breeches with its 2 petals found commonly in rich deciduous forests everywhere. Except for the color, they reminded us country boys of the bleeding hearts our grandmother grew.

There is no doubt that plants with 3 leaves or petals are most common although the individual plant may be rare. The exquisite pink lady's slipper orchid (aka moccasin flower) with its 3 leaves and 1 blossom flourishes on the farm in an area about the size of a small room. Strangely, my mother told us where we would find them and when. The red trillium, which blooms before the white variety, is found in scattered patches throughout most deciduous forests. Not only were we counters of leaves and blooms we were sniffers of everything. Yet the foul odor of rotten meat from the red trillium was both a surprise and a mystery.

Pink Lady's Slipper   Red Trillium

The woods are wide and full of wonders, but we boys were mere counters, nibblers, and sniffers at her mysteries. Just two skinny lads roaming fields like foxes searching for whatever we could find. Here a quartz rock, there an emerald snake, and over there a woodcock's nest.

I have recounted how my cousin and I had stumbled upon some terms in the Fibonacci sequence by counting flower petals. As noted, however, we didn't discover the simple rule for finding the next term by adding the preceding two. You could say, perhaps, that we had no vision of this famous sequence. But you would be wrong. Be it ever so humble we did have a theory of sorts—an idea about what the next term might be before we actually found it. We noticed something curious concerning these numbers: an even (E) is "always" followed by two odds (O). We were generalizing beyond the evidence. See for yourself:

1	1	2	3	5	8	13	21	34	55	89* ...
O	O	E	O	O	E	O	O	E	O	O ...

On the occasions when we applied this knowledge of odds and evens, it was confirmed. In effect, we were predicting the future based on the past, something science has always done. Our little theory was as much a creation as a sonnet by a fledgling poet.

How does nature mold such order out of chaos? This is the question of the ages. In the city, you can see order everywhere, from roads to buildings to street signs, but in the fields and forest signs of order are deep and elusive. Yet a little inspection of nature's fabric shows subtle and beautiful patterns. So what is the purpose of all these Fibonacci spirals and their numbers, and how did they come to be?

It is estimated that 99.9 percent of all species that have ever existed are now extinct. And all these extinct species have one thing in common: they did not leave copies of their DNA, be they seeds, eggs, or babies. As for the plants, a Fibonacci spiral is the best method to pack seeds closely. There you have it:

---

* Therefore, the next term should be even and it is 55 + 89 or 144 (E).

the explanation as to why this Fibonacci frenzy, this exquisite pattern, fills nature's fields with the beauty of art and the designs of mathematics. It's all a matter of *maximizing the seed head through close packing.*

The plant, of course, knows nothing of Fibonacci spirals or numbers. Evolution has put it on a close-packing quest: produce more seeds, have more progeny, be fruitful and multiply, or perish. When only a tiny portion of all your offspring (DNA) survives, it pays to produce hundreds, even thousands or tens of thousands, of copies. Consider the salmon and the dandelion, the sunflower and the pinecone, the daisy and the milkweed.

Milkweed Seeds—The Next Generation

The world of the living tolerates slight variations, while larger ones are punishable by death. In every ecological niche, life hovers around a cluster of particular behaviors and bodily adaptations. The mechanism that brought about these adaptations is the master narrative of the 20th century. As philosopher Daniel Dennett says, "If I were to give an award for the single best idea anyone has ever had, I'd give it to Darwin, ahead of Newton or Einstein." He wasn't referring to evolution, which had been discussed since the time of the Greeks. Even Darwin's grandfather, Erasmus, wrote about evolution—an idea as firmly established as the Earth rotating around the sun. No, Darwin's dangerous idea was the discovery of the *mechanism for evolution*, the force that causes descent with modification and the force that brings order out of chaos. We call it *natural selection*.

All creatures, great and small, dance upon this edge of life. Any variance too far and all is lost. From womb to tomb, this is our passage—no broad primrose path for us. In his lyrical "Ode to the West Wind," Shelley rages against these constraints comparing human limitations to the freedom of the wind:

Wild Spirit, which art moving everywhere;
Destroyer and preserver; hear, O, hear!
. . . .
Oh, lift me as a wave, a leaf, a cloud!
I fall upon the thorns of life! I bleed!

A heavy weight of hours has chain'd and bow'd
One too like thee: tameless, and swift, and proud

Starflower

Near the small area where the pink lady's slipper grows is a wider region of flowers with 7 petals—a number not in our sequence. This wasn't an 8-petal flower with a fallen one; every new flower had exactly 7 petals, although the top flower (pictured here) has already lost a petal. Starflowers are one of the few plants that typically have 7 petals, yet this number can vary from 5 to 10. They also have 7 leaves. Count them!

Our grandmother was far too old to scramble through the woods to the edge of the cranberry bog where these flowers grew abundantly so we brought her one. "Starflower," she said proudly, and told us where we had picked it. Evidently, she had once been a young girl exploring the land as we now did.

Observations verify that more than 90 percent of all plants worldwide display Fibonacci numbers. This is a confirmation of the consistency my cousin and I had found. But in nature multiple forces are always at work, so outcomes tend to be a little messy. What about the starflower and the four-leaf clover? What about the remaining 10 percent? That's still an enormous quantity of plant species. I once grew a sunflower with 29 spirals one

Four-Leaf Clover

way and 47 the other, which broke the Fibonacci pattern. I replanted some of its seeds to learn what numbers I might get in the next generation, but a busy squirrel ate them all.

Because there are exceptions to the Fibonacci sequence, we have the following two choices:

- Throw all the numbers in the waste basket, or
- Find a larger theory that includes the Fibonacci numbers and the exceptions.

Science is more a journey than a destination, so I opted for the second choice. My cousin and I were not wrong in our ob-

Dandelion Seed Head: 21/34

servations, just incomplete. To finish this investigation, however, would take us beyond the scope of this book. For those who are interested, I have explored this larger theory in a new book titled *Immortal Ideas: Shared by Art, Science, and Nature.* Readers should consult the sixth chapter, "Numbers: Natural" for all the details.

Close-Packed Seed Head of a Sunflower: 34/55

The Fibonacci sequence is the grain in the stone, the path in the forest, the long sought after pattern for the consistency we would-be Pythagoreans had blundered upon in the dreamtime of our youth. And so we began to know this place for the first time.

CHAPTER—12

A MISCELLANY OF BIRDS

The bluebird carries the sky on his back.
Henry David Thoreau, *Journals*, April 3, 1852

When we left paradise, we moved to the city and lived with one of my mother's sisters. Mother had five sisters although one died on Christmas Eve at the age of twenty. Like all farm families—it didn't matter that we lived in the city—we were close, very close. My city aunt was alone in the house so she welcomed my mother's company. This was World War II and her husband was in Europe on the Italian Front. She was alone but for her two children, a boy and his older sister. My city cousin was four years my senior so we didn't do much together; he had friends of his own.

In my memory, I was always sick in the city with a cold or the flu or some other malady. Instead of forests and fields, I had a bed and a postage-stamp lawn. My mother labored in a downtown sweatshop sewing skirts on piecework, while my aunt toiled in a paint factory at the end of our working-class street. No one complained, ever! It was February and I was in bed plastered with cold sores and miserable. But my aunt would walk home during her lunch to attend to my misery and make me soup and a sandwich. The best day I ever had in the city was about to happen.

While trudging up the back lane through the blinding snow and freezing cold, my aunt picked up something struggling and barely alive in a snowdrift. To warm this creature, she put it under her thin coat and brought it home to cheer me. I heard the front door open, but she didn't come upstairs directly. She was searching for a small cardboard box before she ascended the stairs with her surprise. Slowly I lifted a corner of the box to reveal a common pigeon in some distress, lying on its side. Right away I gave it part of my homemade muffin from the side table. *It ate!* My aunt said it was "snow blind"—neither she nor I had any idea what this "common" bird would bring to our lives.

The Common Pigeon

After my aunt trekked back to work, I got out of bed because I had a patient to attend to. From the kitchen I retrieved a glass and filled it with water. This bird drank like a horse, head down and sucking it in. All the birds I had known trapped a little water in the mouth and then tilted their heads back to let it trickle down their throats.

When my city cousin got home from school, he suggested we build a little pigeon coop in the basement. He was always good with construction. By the following morning my patient seemed fully recovered. We decided to call him "common," but he turned out to be anything but.

That's how it all started. On weekends we would walk downtown to the farmer's market and buy special pigeons, tipplers, tumblers, rollers, homers, and racers. A few market sellers had strange pigeons (*see* photo) they called "fancies" with unusual bodies and plumage. We didn't like them and instinctively felt they wouldn't do well with our mostly backstreet birds. Pigeons have a strict pecking order, and we were certain that "common" was top bird.

Fancy Pigeon: Pouter

All the birds we bought went into the basement, which was beginning to have an odor all its own. Since our pigeon coop was becoming large, we built an outside extension that the birds could access through a basement window. They ate a lot; they ate everything. Eventually, we opened the door of the outside cage and let them go free. They loved to fly in groups, circling high in the city sky. They must have thought the city was built for them for they were rock doves whose ancestors lived in canyons and rested and bred on ledges similar to the city's roofs and windowsills. After every flight they relaxed on some nearby roof, but eventually they came home to their coop because it had the free food. Occasionally, they arrived with a new hungry friend. We were getting a large flock; who knew where it might end.

Well we soon found out! That June my uncle arrived home from the war—it was a joyous occasion, but things were about to change. I'm certain he thought the entire house was being transformed into a pigeon coop. We were ordered to get rid of the birds, all the birds, and their smelly coops. I suggested we take them to the farm, and we did. My country uncle was agreeable to our passion, and his son was thrilled, so the birds took over the loft of one of the many barns, all 40 or more including the original pigeon we called "common."

Some of the barns were constructed of logs; others were post and beam. By that, I mean a skeleton of large squared white-pine beams was erected first and boards nailed on later. The pigeon barn was post and beam, and these timbers were perfect cliffs for roosting and nesting, or so my country cousin and I hoped. My older cousin from the city never stayed long on the farm; his main concern in life was earning money.

The lower level of this barn was the domain of pigs, particularly old sows and their piglets. When I was a boy on the farm, there came a time for the castration of the piglets. My uncle would duly equip himself with his straight razor for the surgery and turpentine for the antiseptic. My cousin and I *never* went into the barn to witness this ghastly business. The ear-piercing squeals from the diminished piglets plus our wild imaginations were sufficient reality for us. Occasionally a calf would be castrated, and one time an unmanageable bull had a tight elastic band put around the top of his scrotum until his testes and his temper both atrophied. Geldings, capons, oxen, and so on are all castrati, the operation done for taste and obedience.

Castration is such a permanent condition. Not only is the sexual drive greatly weakened but also the genetic line is virtually extinguished. By selective breeding—unnatural selection—we subdue the wild element in animals and make them placid and pliable to our wishes. Beyond even this, we dehorn, debud, and declaw. We use gelding, spaying, castrating, sterilizing, neutering, fixing, emasculating, or any other action, surgical, chemical, or otherwise, to emasculate, to castrate. We will be masters of the beasts. Man will have dominion over the other animals!

Country pigeons are different from city pigeons. Our birds soon went wild. We could no longer approach them even with food. And although we never saw a "hen hawk" take a hen, they did kill pigeons. The night also had its own predators—weasels, raccoons, and skunks, or so we were told.

By climbing a ladder nailed to an interior wall of the barn housing the pigeons, we could ascend to the floor of the loft, which had a layer of old hay. Sitting quietly, we observed "our" pigeons for any signs of nest building. We did this every day until it finally happened. The pigeon we called "common" was bringing pieces of nesting material to what must clearly be his mate. We were more excited than the parents to be.

Just as my mother had many sisters, my father had even more brothers. The oldest seems to have been the only one to avoid the hazards of alcoholism—most of the others met tragic ends. This uncle was a pigeon fancier, by that I mean he kept a barn full of odd breeds (*see* "Fancy Pigeons") like the ones in the city market. From him my cousin and I learned most of what we knew about pigeons. He told us "The male will bring the female *one stick* at a time for their nest." We were amazed at the varieties of these birds and had no explanation for it. I doubt we thought of it.

Fancy Pigeons

Someone did think about it, however, and that someone thought long and hard and these thoughts filled the first two chapters of his epic book *On the Origin of Species**. After reading these initial chapters, Darwin's editor thought the entire book was about pigeons. The naturalist set up an elaborate pigeon coop at Down House, his home in Kent County, buying pigeons

---

* Biologists define species as the largest group of organisms capable of interbreeding and producing fertile offspring.

of 16 different breeds to perform his artificial selection experiments. His children were fascinated because breeding pigeons was a wonderful improvement over the eight years their father had spent dissecting barnacles. In 1855, Darwin wrote to his friend Charles Lyell, who was planning a visit:

> I hope Lady Lyell & yourself will remember whenever you want a little rest & have time how very glad we should be to see you here. I will show you my pigeons! Which is the greatest treat, in my opinion, which can be offered to human beings.

It's clear that in the 1850s pigeons were an admired bird. As noted, Darwin's children fell in love with pigeons. Years later, his daughter Henrietta wrote the following:

> I can still recall their different characteristics: a cross old fantail who in taking food from my hand liked to give a good peck & hurt me if he could. The pouter pigeon was good-natured but not clever, and I remember a hen Jacobin which I considered rather feeble-minded.

On the farm surrounded by hundreds of animals and birds, it was obvious that each had a different personality. At our peril, we approached certain geese, turkeys, sows, and boars. Others were friendly. One hen was very tame, so much so that my cousin and I called her "pet" hen. (We were not inventive in our naming.) We often picked her up and walked around the barnyard; when we played with her chicks, she was equally well tempered.

Jacobin Fancy

Plain

You might ask what Darwin learned from his intense study of pigeons. Well the answer is a lot more than from the Galapagos finches. First he showed that all this phenomenal variety, in appearance and behavior, was derived from the wild pigeon—the one my aunt brought home to cheer a sick boy. Victorians didn't think there was sufficient variety in any species to be important. Indeed, pigeon breeders believed the same and supposed all their varieties were the descendants of eight or nine different species, not one. They certainly did not imagine descent from the street pigeon. Darwin's research proved otherwise and further implied that every wild creature held immense variety in what we today would call its genetic code. And for evolution to do its work, it needs this variety.

Not satisfied with just this discovery, the naturalist proved that the entire process of artificial selection can be reversed—these fancy pigeons can be bred to look like street pigeons again through artificial selection. We have come full circle! Selection harbors immense power whether *artificial*, which works quickly, or *natural*, which requires vast periods of time.

> *On the first part of the journey,*
> *I was looking at all the life.*
> *There were plants and birds and rocks and things.*
> *There was sand and hills and rings.*
> "A Horse with No Name" a song by Dewey Bunnell

I arrived in paradise on July 1, and was cast out on Labor Day in September. Each summer mother took my clothes to my room in the house with two staircases and the stuffed owl. But I ran to the barnyard pond to see the hundreds of tadpoles eating algae from the rocks. Then on to the hollow fence post near the road to check on the bluebirds' nest. I was never disappointed.

Male Eastern Bluebird

Bluebirds appear to be models of family values. In the spring they are always working together to raise their family. Occasionally, young birds from the first brood will return to help raise the second. Once, when a female died, the male successfully raised five babies as a single parent. When you hear the bluebird's gentle song in the springtime and see him sitting on a fencepost, your spirit rises and your mood brightens.

Six Baby Bluebirds   Fledgling

The female bluebird is in charge. Her mate will show her possible nesting sites (cavities), but she makes the final decision. A hollow fence post, however, seems a poor choice: it's open to the rain and a forearm's distance for the fledglings to scramble up, but they do. The nest was successful year after year, yet when my aunt and uncle abandoned the farm so did the bluebirds.

In the baby bluebird nest (*see* photo) you will find no feces or urine. The young excrete a fecal sac, which the diligent parents immediately remove; this keeps the nest clean and healthy. And parents will feed the fledgling on the ground (pictured here) until he is fully airborne. They will never abandon him.

If you remove a few babies from the nest and check their legs and bodies, you often discover parasitic maggots attached (blowfly larvae). Remove these and replace the entire nest if possible. You can quickly fashion a fresh nest from nearby grasses. Surprisingly none of this permanently disturbs the parents who immediately return to the nest on your departure. I once had a mother bluebird land on my hand as I returned her last baby. Foolishly, I almost felt she knew what I was doing.

Although my cousin and I collected bird's eggs, we never touched the bluebird nest in the fence post. Had we done so our grandmother would have taken her broom to us. As previously noted, she knew a thing or two about beauty, and we learned from her. It is little wonder this is the bird of legend and myth. We ignorant farm boys understood without ever hearing the song "Bluebird of Happiness." We knew without ever having heard Judy Garland sing "Somewhere over the rainbow /Bluebirds fly" from the immortal *Wizard of Oz*. This bird touches our deepest feelings, and, as long as it is with us, somehow, we know the world is still all right.

In and about the barns and the fields the bluebird has a competitor and a companion, the swallow. Although, according to Thoreau, "The bluebird carries the sky on his back," the sky itself belongs to the swallows. They sweep and roll with such heedless abandon and with a grace unmatched by any other bird. My cousin and I have often seen a barn swallow swoop under the lowest strand of a wire fence. They routinely careen into the barn through a vertical crack in the boards that would have wedged our hand. The barn swallows are all gone now—retreated to the more southerly regions of our province. Only their ancient mud nests still cling to the beams of the old barn the way the Anasazi adobe homes clutch the cliffs of the Canyon de Chelly. But every year, tree swallows

Barn Swallow

return to my bird boxes. They eat as they fly, flashing their metal-lic-blue backs and milky-white breasts. Over Walden and Walk-er's Pond, they also nest in woodpecker's holes, but their true domain is heaven's high vault.

Tree Swallow

Without perfect eye-wing coordination, swallows would be quickly selected out of the breeding population. Natural selection must have acted harshly and instantly in their evolution. Their way of life leaves no room for error, nor have I ever seen them make one.

Bird Entrance in Barn

When the pigeons took occu-pancy of the post-and-beam barn, the resident barn swallows changed buildings. Both birds entered through the ornate en-trance, but only the pigeons used the landing pad (*see* photo). After "common" pigeon's mate built her nest, she laid two eggs, but they shared incubation duties. He took the day shift, she the night. Our excitement mounted with each day! The eggs hatched after about three weeks, but the summer was already half over for me. It's hopeless now for me to comprehend the depth of feeling my cousin and I had for these baby birds. They were our children, and I needed to see them fledge *before* Labor Day.

As boys, we did not know every bird on the farm; as an adult, I still don't. Nature holds many surprises; she has had a billion years to prepare them.

Decades after those sunny summer days, my cousin was helping me finish my cabin on the back 40 acres of the farm. It was early spring, damp as I recall, and we had stopped to make a pot (can) of tea. This wasn't easy because we had neither fire nor water. We dipped a can to get *black* water from a nearby vernal pond, surely full of microscopic life, "for the protein" and long boiled it over a makeshift tripod fire.

As we were doing this, another much older cousin arrived. (It would seem I had cousins to spare.) He was the son of the woman with the goiter and mother's only brother, and we rarely saw him. He grew up in the original single-story farmhouse, long since burned down, near the only existing barn. "Would you like some fresh spring leeks to go with your 'protein' tea?" he asked. We nodded affirmatively.

An hour or so later, he returned with a bag of these spring delicacies. We three drank black tea, ate fresh leeks, and laughed at life. We were not living off the fat of the land; this land had no fat, and almost no lean. Both of these cousins died young, but I remember that morning as if we had dined on ambrosia and sipped nectar.

American Woodcock on Nest

This cousin, while returning from picking leeks, had almost stepped on a remarkably camouflaged bird sitting on her nest (*see* photograph of the nesting American woodcock). To be certain of locating it again, he left his scarf as a marker on a nearby bush. Even so, it took us some time to find this nest. It was an American woodcock sitting on her four eggs, a rare find. Since that day, I have never found another.

Fishworm Hunter   Got it!

The woodcock only *appears* to have been put together by a dysfunctional committee. Rather, the bird is the result of natural selection over millennia. Truly evolution, the Blind Watchmaker, has fashioned a most bizarre bird. Its elaborate courtship flight at dusk, during which it rises in widening circles, zigzags back to earth, and calls with a nasal "peent, peent, peent" sound, can rival the mating performance of any New Guinea bird of paradise.

When the eggs hatch, the chicks run away within an hour or two, just as chickens do. Life on the forest floor is dangerous. On moonlit nights in the summer, I have seen the hen woodcock with her brood of bouncy clowns moving secretly through my orchard. With enormous bills and bobbing walk, they are a wondrous sight. As with robins, and for the same reasons, woodcocks like rainy days. My grandmother colorfully called them "timberdoodles," and they were frequently in her garden on wet mornings.

Because I am an advocate for evolution by natural selection, creationists occasionally confront me. With respect to birds they always say, "How does a creature without wings suddenly get them?" "What good is half a wing?"

But of course, getting wings isn't sudden, nor is any other change. That's why it is called "evolution." And a tenth, a hundredth, even a thousandth of a wing is better than no wing, especial-

Blue Jay in Winter

ly if you are using it for warmth as northern birds regularly do. The blue jay pictured here has puffed out his feathers to have extra layers of insulation around his body. He can't do as we do and wear a heavier coat. Turkeys use their wings as umbrellas to keep themselves and their babies dry. In the case of the woodcock, her feathers provide the spectacular advantage of near perfect camouflage. The classic step in wing evolution is gliding. If you can glide from one tree to another to escape a predator, you live another day. Many, many creatures, including lizards, frogs, snakes, and mammals, have evolved to glide. On the farm, we have two aerial mammals, one is a glider the other a flyer; we'll see this mysterious glider in the next chapter. Creationists, however, discount connections between flyers and gliders. Indeed, they have long since stopped listening to reason. Theirs is an unshakeable *belief* rather than a conclusion arrived at from evidence.

Feathers may well have evolved for any number of reasons before the jump to gliding and flying. First you glide, then you fly. Analogously, the nose evolved for smelling, but it has proven itself well suited to hold up our eyeglasses. Some feature that evolved for a specific purpose is often useful elsewhere. Who has not used a knife as a screwdriver?

Through the forests and over the fields of this harsh land lives an elfin creature, seldom seen and rarely heard. On the south side of the mill house, my mother planted flowers; this was near where I found the unfortunate puff adder. Something metallic with flashes of dark red the size of a large insect was hovering around these flowers. Mother said they were hummingbirds. I never saw another for three decades.

Male Ruby-Throated Hummingbird

With the help of my cousin, the cabin was finally finished, so I decided to mount a hummingbird feeder. I filled the glass contraption with a dense mixture of sugar and water. Placing it on the deck, I stood on a chair to screw a hook into an overhanging beam from which to hang the feeder. While standing on the chair I was astonished to see a hummingbird already sipping nectar. From this auspicious start, things went uphill. Soon I had a dozen or more of these little darters, and this was only early May. Wait, I thought, until they arrive with their babies, and they did

The Eagle Has Landed: Juvenile Male

by August. Why had I not seen these beauties for so long? Perhaps because they fly so quickly they can be mistaken for bumblebees or clearwing hummingbird moths, or more likely, I wasn't truly looking.

Clearwing on Lilac   Clearwing on Milkweed

Hummingbirds occur only in the Americas, but the farm has just a single species, the ruby-throated. Unlike insects, they will sip nectar from flowers, and incidentally pollinate these plants, even when it rains. Perhaps that's one of the reasons there are over 300 different species in the wet tropics: plants need them. Some of these birds have evolved to pollinate just a few or even a single type of flower. Such specialization is dangerous in a changing environment; the ruby-throat is a generalist.

Hummingbird on Bee Balm

In Europe and India, the sunbird plays a role analogous to that of the hummingbird. Sunbirds are larger and less elegant, but they get the job done. By the nature of their employment, different species that survive using the same methods evolve to look alike. Biologists call this process convergent evolution, the independent evolution of similar features in species of different lineages. Compare the woodchuck, a mammal of North America, to the wombat, a marsupial of Australia. They look like close cousins, but they are extremely distant on the evolutionary tree of life. Their "job descriptions," however, would be identical: stubborn loner wanted to build impressive burrow and consume tender young plants. Closer to home, swallows and swifts look like twins—they both catch insects on the wing—but they are on quite different branches of life's tree.

When the ruby-throats arrive at the farm, usually in the first week of May, there are extremely few flowers. And those that are in bloom are small and almost without nectar. This is when being a generalist is advantageous. These little gem-like birds follow the yellow-bellied sapsucker, a type of woodpecker, who taps trees to drink the sap and eat insects trapped by this sticky liquid (*see* the rows of sap holes in the pictured birch tree). Hummingbirds benefit from this largesse because tree sap is similar to plant nectar and the insects are a protein bonus.

Yellow-Bellied Sapsucker

Yellow-bellied sapsuckers time themselves to arrive when the sap is running, and the ruby-throats trail them. So during these lean spring days, they get along with a little help from their friends.

Pictured here is a miscellany of eight birds. Two deserve special comment. On summer evenings, when my cousin and I were surrounded by dark forests and warm cows, a, flute-like song warbled us shoeless shepherds home. We never saw the singer.

Hermit Thrush   Rose-Breasted Grosbeak

White-Breasted Nuthatch   Red-Breasted Nuthatch

Chestnut-Sided Warbler   Downy Woodpecker

American Tree Sparrow   Chickadee

It was decades before I discovered this song was the ballad of the secretive hermit thrush. What this thrush does for your ears, the rose-breasted grosbeak does for your eyes; it is certainly one of America's most gorgeous birds.

Charles Darwin proved that all the different breeds of pigeons are descendants of a single species, the rock dove. By *artificial selection*, from so simple a beginning, endless forms most beautiful and bizarre have been and are being bred.

Worldwide there are about 10,000 different species of bird. In these few pages, we have merely lifted the corner of the cardboard box to peek inside. This is my feeble effort to know the place for the first time. Scientists have compelling evidence that all this profusion of feather and song is descended from a single species that lived in the Late Jurassic period. Just two years after the publication of *On the Origin of Species*, an exquisite fossil, transitional from dinosaur to bird, was discovered in Germany and named *Archaeopteryx*[*]. It had jaws and sharp teeth, three fingers with claws, and a long bony tail; it also had feathers and a wishbone. Since this find, even earlier "birds" have been unearthed in China. By *natural selection* "from so simple a beginning endless forms most beautiful and most wonderful have been, and are being, evolved."

In the summer months, we had little concept of time; there were no clocks that I recall. But, as I remember the day, the tadpoles had left the pond, the bluebirds had fledged from the fence post,

---

[*] To see this fossil, search "*Archaeopteryx*."

and the baby pigeons were maturing. These were the only clocks I watched. By now the pigeons were familiar with our presence in the barn and remained undisturbed even when we scaled the timbers to better view the nest, which was just below their entrance.

When the day arrived for me to leave, my two pigeons still had not fledged. I stood uncomfortably in the barnyard in strange clothes and shoes. The ground felt hard. A bag of my meager belongings was hanging from my arm. The air was hot and humid; I started to pant. The adults were fussing about, doing the things they always do and saying their goodbyes. My father started the car, eager, as always, to depart. Just at that moment, I saw the pigeon called "common" on the roof of the post-and-beam barn leaning over to look at the bird entrance. Almost as he did, one of the babies stepped out onto the platform. I knew it was going to fly; no one else but my cousin realized what was happening. "Get in," I was told, but I didn't move. A more emphatic "get in" reached my ears but I could barely hear.

At that moment, I started to sing one of my grandmother's favorite songs "We'll all go together up through the blooming heather." Everyone stared at me, I suspect, but I saw only the peak of the barn with the moment of truth for this fledgling. I continued to sing and grandmother joined me. My cousin joined as well for he somehow knew he should. My mother, realizing this was an extraordinary moment, told my father, "Your son needs you to wait." And he did. Shortly the second bird joined the first on the platform; then they both flew to the roof of the horse barn nearer us, where "common" pigeon joined them. My birds were free!

We drove away. That fall, my aunt and uncle abandoned the farm, and I never spent another summer with them in paradise. After this, I became the keeper of memories.

POSTSCRIPT: That Thanksgiving weekend my mother and I returned to the farm to help my aunt and uncle pack up. All the animals had been sold or given away, and the pigeons had been eaten or scared away by predators—a weasel it was said.

But I found "common" pigeon sitting alone on the roof of the post-and-beam barn. Apparently, he was the sole survivor. My cousin and his parents drove away in an open-top truck while my mother and I returned to the city. The farm with the two staircases and the stuffed owl was forsaken and "common" pigeon left to an unknown future.

CHAPTER—13

THE FIFTH SQUIRREL

The force that through the green fuse drives the flower
Drives my green age; that blasts the roots of trees
Is my destroyer.
And I am dumb to tell the crooked rose
My youth is bent by the same wintry fever.
Dylan Thomas, "The Force that through the Green Fuse Drives the Flower"

We gave chase to this "rare" animal, a black squirrel, only the second of its species I had seen. The forest was open with few trees, so it jumped into a pile of leaves enclosed by a tree stump. I brushed the leaves aside and saw its quivering back arched high. Instinctively I grasped the creature, for I had a need to touch the truly wild. My cousin had more sense. The sinewy muscles pulsed through my hand and up my arm, as it twisted around to bite me. "Go free," I shouted and released my grip. As boys, we never saw another black squirrel on the farm. In the decades that followed, I've seen only six more on the property.

Gray Squirrel   Black Squirrel

Squirrels are the city's most often seen wild mammal, and, like pigeons, they are generally loathed. "Tree rats" I've heard them called. Although mice and raccoons are also plentiful in urban areas, they are seldom seen. Black and gray squirrels are the same species; both colors occur in littermates. Yet all squirrels in our area are *black* whether from the mill, farm, or town, and they are rare, very rare.

I was a child when I saw my first black squirrel at the lumber mill. One of them regularly entered the horse barn through the solid plank door to eat any leftover oats in the feed bins. In this barn, our gentle dog Queenie had a manger full of puppies. As a young "hunter," I was determined to capture this thieving squirrel. One day as it entered the barn through the door, I circled around and slammed the door shut. Mission accomplished! Now what? I had no next step, so the squirrel eventually left the barn stuffed with oats.

My cousin and I wondered why we never saw another black squirrel or its gray sibling. We did have four other squirrel species on the farm, although one of these was unknown to us. Studies show that the darker you are the more of the sun's heat you absorb in the wintertime; deer have darker coats from November to April, for example. Certainly, the black squirrel's coat is an advantage for heat retention. That may explain why we have no gray squirrels. But why don't we have any black?

The initial photographs in this chapter hold the answer. To me, and hopefully to the reader, the black squirrel stands out boldly while the gray squirrel's outline is less apparent and blends with the tree. Yet it's not just the color, it's how the colors are distributed. The black squirrel is *black* all over, but the gray has a white belly, which helps break up its outline. Many creatures—mammals, birds, fish, reptiles, insects, even the family dog—have white under parts.

Biologists call this *countershading* and it's a form of camouflage; the animal is darker on the upper side and lighter on the underside of the body. This pattern has existed since at least the Cretaceous period (approximately 145 to 65 million years ago). Richard Dawkins, in his memoir *An Appetite for Wonder*, maintains countershading allows the wearer to appear flat or empty and hence of no food value.

Consider the two photographs of moon craters (courtesy of NASA). The one on the left is empty, and the one on the right is a solid mound. This, however, is a well-known optical illusion. Please turn this page upside down. Voila! The situation is reversed: the empty crater becomes the mound and vice versa. Looking closely reveals these are identical photographs of the Webb crater rotated 180° relative to each other. The left crater is countershaded (dark top, light bottom) and, as Dawkins says, it appears empty. The right crater is reverse-countershaded and appears full. In large part, the reason most but not all creatures great and small have white bellies is to take advantage of countershading.

A White-Bellied Squirrel

My cousin and I had BB guns, and we were excellent shots. On occasion, we shot at red squirrels but killed chipmunks, and I am ashamed to remember, we skinned them. My father killed and skinned red squirrels for profit; we had no such excuse. After the skinning and drying, we stored them with our snake-skins in the bottom drawer of our bedroom dresser. When my mother unexpectedly happened upon our collection of skins, the result was a loud string of %!:#!&@!! followed by the slamming of the drawer. We admired the whiteness of these squirrels' bellies (*see* photo), so pure, so perfect. But this admiration gave us no pause for thought or sympathy. That came later.

| Skunk | Porcupine |

"This is the exception that proves the rule" was never more appropriate than in reverse countershading. In this situation, natural selection has worked its magic to make the animal more visible as a *warning sign*. Any animal that issues such a warning needs a strong defense system to back up its bravado. The skunk and porcupine (pictured here) have such mechanisms. These two animals not only have black bellies but also have white fur or quills on their backs. You can't miss them, but you should. Recall the young bear (Chapter 5) with quills in her face. Skunks and porcupines do not run away; they stand and deliver.

Black squirrels have no countershading, and they have no special defenses for being so obvious. Hence, they are vulnerable to the farm's numerous predators: foxes, wolves, bears, fishers, mink, hawks, and eagles. I maintain this is the reason they can't survive on our farm, but they do rather well in town with its few predators. This theory is without hard data. It may be that the smaller but hyperactive red squirrels just beat the crap out of their black cousins.

Woodchuck in Springtime (April 10)

The woodchuck is our largest squirrel. He can climb trees if the occasion requires it, but, as his other name—groundhog—implies, he prefers to touch the earth. Robert Frost commemorates this member of the squirrel family in his poem "A Drumlin Woodchuck." Here are two stanzas:

> *My own strategic retreat*
> *Is where two rocks almost meet,*
> *And still more secure and snug,*
> *A two-door burrow I dug.*
>
> *All we who prefer to live*
> *Have a little whistle we give,*
> *And flash, at the least alarm*
> *We dive down under the farm.*

Woodchucks are one of the farm's true hibernators. The animal sleeps away winter's terrible hardship, taking only a single breath every six minutes and maintaining a body temperature of 3° C. He appears dead. Yet, his photograph—taken in April during the first days of the spring—reveals an animal in good condition just out of hibernation. We forget how amazing hibernation truly is! It's very like "stasis" from the *Star Trek* franchise, the state in which someone passes great periods of time totally unaware in a special chamber. Any unfortunate woodchuck brought out of stasis for amusement on February 2 knows that, whether he sees his shadow or a dinosaur, there will be six more weeks of winter in Canada. Natural selection created hibernation as a perfect method to escape the ravages of winter. With this gift plus his warning whistles to littermates and the ability to climb trees or go to earth to escape danger, this squirrel appears not to need countershading, and, indeed, he has none.

Upward Facing Chuck   Downward Facing Chuck

After a long winter's nap—about six months—our woodchuck does some yoga. He hibernated curled up in a tight ball so it must have felt good to stretch. This session lasted some time, with the woodchuck repeating various positions over and over.

My cousin and I decided to catch a woodchuck without using a damaging leg-hold trap—no easy task. We equipped ourselves with a burlap bag and a shovel. Locating one of their burrows was easy; locating one we might possibly dig out was not. We made our choice by selecting a burrow on top of exposed Precambrian shield, trusting it wasn't very deep. After blocking his exit hole with a granite boulder, we took turns digging for what seemed hours. Our soft hands soon developed blisters, but we didn't stop. We wrapped them in rags as makeshift gloves and continued digging. Ultimately our excavation approached the boulder—just a forearm's length to go and still no sign of our ground squirrel. But he was there squeezed up tightly against the boulder. I could see his back legs! My cousin held the burlap bag open while, with a continuous motion, I pulled him out by his hind legs and dropped him in. We had our woodchuck.

We had prepared a large wooden crate lined with straw for his home. The pigs reluctantly shared their mash plus we put in an armful of fresh garden greens. By the next morning, however, he had gnawed an exit hole, and that ended our career in raising woodchucks. It's significant that no one since has attempted this form of animal husbandry. Some of our poorer neighbors ate them and judged the meat delicious. Our family did not.

Right after My Nap, I'll Move this Rock.

The adult world considered our woodchuck catching pure foolishness, and perhaps it was. But these adventures stand out clearly in my memory when a thousand others deemed notable by the adult world are gone. Who judges importance? Who fixes value? We two boys had slipped the shackles of time for a day, and, like two bears, we dug out a groundhog. The fact that he soon escaped was a good thing. My cousin and I judged all this as important—I still do.

The chipmunk is our smallest squirrel, the exquisite result of long evolution. That's why we killed and skinned them. We needed to possess their beauty. For us morality and beauty were unconnected; perhaps they always are. If we had cameras, we could have gathered all this wonder without causing death.

Today when I shoot an animal, nothing dies. In retrospect it seems most of our activities were in pursuit of beauty: the birds, the flowers, the animals, their skins, our pigeons, our collection of bird's eggs, really the entire panoply of farm life. That's why, as mentioned previously, we were captivated by a small calendar of colorful bird pictures. We were primitives. My cousin kept banty roosters just because their plumage was flamboyant and for no other reason. As evidence of one of the Blind Watchmaker's most gorgeous creations, life presents the chipmunk:

A Survivor in a Jurassic World

For this miniature ground squirrel, predators are everywhere and they are large, very large. Yet, scientists tell us primordial chipmunks were around 25 million years ago—incredibly longer than humans have existed. Their hoarding instinct points to a genetic fear of starvation; in one summer they will store enough food for years, although on average they live fewer than two. They are not true hibernators; if they were, they wouldn't hoard food. During winter blizzards, they wake up at regular intervals, enjoy a snack and a bathroom break, and fall back to sleep in their snug dens under a carpet of snow. In later years after my cousin had left me, I tamed these creatures. Because of our size difference, it's as if a *T. rex* were playing with them. With other chipmunks, however, they are aggressive and territorial.

Chipmunk at His Plunge Hole

These elfin gems were architects of one of the farm's most enduring mysteries, one my cousin and I never solved. Several times every summer, we would find small mounds of fine soil free of stones and sticks. We searched diligently for the hole of the animal who constructed this pile but we never found it nor, I suspect, did predators. Years later, I discovered the answer. After making this mound, the chipmunk plugs the hole in favor of an inconspicuous "plunge" entrance some distance away—a simple, elegant survival trick.

When so many species are in distress and declining, the chipmunk still thrives. He has only a few tricks and an incredible work ethic, but that would seem to be enough.

My cousin and I lived in a special time of abundant life. In the fields, the forests, the skies, the lakes, and the ponds, even in our home, wildlife was everywhere. We were like Audubon, who must have thought the supply of birds was endless, for he killed every bird he painted. We saw no end of songbirds, snakes, turtles, frogs, deer, and so on. But where have all the species gone? Gone to extinction everyone—well almost. To paraphrase Carl Sagan, to get a species back from extinction you must first create the universe.

We left the cabin right after breakfast and turned to the west, away from the bright sunlight reflecting off the snow. Our snow-shoes felt light as we wove through the woods to one of my grandfather's still-open fields. It was a good spot for partridge (ruffed grouse) to dive into the snow forming a warm snow cave for the night. One snow dimple (entrance) implied the partridge was still there; two dimples (exit) meant it had left.

Fox Kill Site

The first thing we found was the carcass of a fox's breakfast. Clearly, this animal knew everything we did about partridge, and he was here by sunrise. At the far end of this field, my friend spotted some of these birds in a yellow birch tree—the lucky survivors (*see* photo).

These birds have a relatively easy time in the winter. Besides the berries, the trees and bushes in northern latitudes all bud in the fall to get a jump on next summer's short growing season, a distinct evolutionary advantage. By far the favorite winter foods for grouse are the buds of the trembling aspen and the yellow birch. Combine this food with warm snow cabins and, despite the odd raiding fox, you have a recipe for success.

Partridge in Yellow Birch Tree

While we were still in the open, I heard the nearby croak, croak, croak of a raven, a bird my cousin and I never knew. It circled low, tilting its head to get a better look at us; surprisingly, it circled even closer a second time. We stared into its black eye and realized another consciousness stared back. This was not the blank, mechanical gaze of a robin but a knowing glance. And the sound of the air rushing through its wings evoked the wild freedom of the great northern forests. Quickly, the moment passed and the raven croaked goodbye and flew away.

The Raven

We entered the forest, and, almost immediately, the loud scolding of a red squirrel greeted us. "What can they possibly find to eat?" my friend asked. "The pinecones provide an abundance of seeds," I replied. Just as the northern finches are the avian seed warriors, the red squirrels are the mammalian, and they cover the same range all round the top of the world. In poor cone years, squirrels eat mostly balsam fir buds (*see* photo) much like the partridge.

Balsam Fir Buds

Red Squirrel Eating Balsam Buds

When my cousin and I were on the farm, we never killed a red squirrel; they are too robust to be taken by a BB gun. I realize now that because of their countershading they are also difficult to see. No forest creature is more energetic or cantankerous. Almost all their lives are spent as bachelors or spinsters, but for the yearly day of estrus. Nonetheless, female red squirrels are excellent providers and caregivers.

My friend and I took turns breaking trail because the snow was deep and soft and our snowshoes were sinking. It was past noon, so we had had some lunch and felt energized. As we pushed up a hill, I said to my friend, "This is no country for old men" or even the middle aged I thought. My cabin on the back 40 acres was about an hour distant, so we would be home soon. The sky was so crystalline clear and blue, cloudless and quiet, we could have been on Neptune. Because of the exertion, our bodies were warm but the cold bit at our noses.

As we reached the crest of the hill, I was astonished to see a second set of snowshoe tracks. Who were these intruders? Then the realization came to me. They were our tracks, and I had led us in a circle—a feat that's the butt of many a joke. Totally disoriented, I stood there perplexed, lost on property I had known for six decades. A strange feeling came over me, a sensation I still recall. Never again did I snowshoe in the winter without a compass. We had been looking for signs of life, and we had found ourselves.

When Darwin published *On the Origin of Species* in 1859, nothing was known about genetics. Just seven years later, however, Gregor Mendel, scientist and Augustinian friar, changed all that, but his profound significance was not recognized until the twentieth century.

Mendel discovered the concept of the gene; he coined the terms "dominant" and "recessive." This accomplishment was quite impressive for someone who failed university and whom his professors labeled "dull" and "unimaginative." Before Mendel, everyone thought traits averaged out. That is, if a short pea plant fertilizes a tall pea plant, the off-

Gregor Mendel

spring will be of *average height*. But that is not the case! He proved that the first generation of pea plants would all be tall— tallness is a dominant factor.

Over seven years Mendel cultivated an incredible 29,000 pea plants. The man had the evidence! Now if the seeds of this second generation (all tall) are planted and the blossoms properly fertilized then, in the third generation, 1 in 4 plants will be short. It was all or nothing, no averaging. And shortness skipped a generation. Traits pass from plants to their offspring in a mathematically predictable way.

This is Mendel's theory backed by a mountain of evidence. Simple! Elegant! Beautiful! Why in the history of humankind had no one else discovered this? Well, the natural world is incredibly complex—too complex for us to unravel cause and effect, unless we are geniuses like Gregor Mendel. His Augustinian order was not altogether pleased with his work on sex and plants; when he died, the monks burned all his papers.

One time, my cousin and I found a nest of baby red squirrels in the farm's oldest log barn, the one that housed the horses. All the barns had a second storey, and it was here in a rotten log that a mother squirrel had made a nest of fine grasses. She was rarely at home when we visited, but her babies were always covered in several inches of fine warm grasses. Hyperactivity in red squirrels starts young because these little fellows did nothing but wiggle and squirm. To us they were beyond cute; they were exquisite and quiet, unlike their parents. As we pulled back the grasses the last time we visited, the young squirrels jumped out and ran off. Perhaps they returned to their nest later, but we didn't. These creations of the Blind Watchmaker were so flawless Mendel would have said, "They are all like peas in a pod."

Newborn Red Squirrels   Two to Three Weeks Old

Nonetheless, on rare occasions the peas in the pod can be different, quite different. Black squirrels are a genetic variation of the gray squirrel called melanistic*, and, as I noted previously, they do not survive well in the Haliburton hinterlands. The opposite of melanism is albinism, a condition in which an animal lacks pigment and is entirely white with pink eyes. Chances of

---

* Melanism is an unusual darkening of body tissues or fur caused by excessive production of melanin, especially as a form of color variation in animals.

survival in this case are even worse than for black squirrels because lack of pigment (melanin) in the eyes results in retina damage, a deadly condition for a tree acrobat.

There is a third way: an animal may be partly white, mostly white, or entirely white but with normal eyes. Biologists call this leucism, and it's more common. The young "white" red squirrel pictured here posed for me in a red maple tree right beside my cabin. As you can see, his eyes are not pink, so he is not an albino.

A Leucistic "White" Red Squirrel

He had at least one sibling that was hairless or appeared to be (*see* photo). Such wild variations did not bode well for their survival. Indeed, both disappeared in a few days—certainly dinner for one of their many predators. Since that time, I have never seen another leucistic squirrel. Life will tolerate mutations, even multiply them, only if they benefit the owner's survival and reproduction—these did neither.

"Hairless" Red Squirrel

Although as boys, my cousin and I never stumbled across any wild animals with signs of leucism (white hair, fur, feathers, or patches), we saw them nonetheless, every day in the barnyard. Some of our pigeons, chickens, and ducks were leucistic, and one of the horses was piebald meaning black with white patches. Domesticated animals being protected and fed can escape much of the pressure of natural selection—just as humans do and thankfully so.

As wild boys were masters of the squirrels. I had laid my hand on the back of a black squirrel and knew its power. We had dug up and bagged a woodchuck like two wild men. Chipmunks had been shot and skinned, and we knew the nursery of red squirrels and much of their rough ways. But something remained—a fifth squirrel no one spoke of. Him we did not know, and it's only after my cousin's death that I learned of this squirrel's reality.

My uncle, who knew much of forest and farm, never hinted at the existence of these squirrels. All the lumberjacks at the mill, who cut down their homes, surely had seen them but remained mute. And my father never mentioned much of anything. This secretive animal is the *northern flying squirrel*, intermediate in size between a chipmunk and a red squirrel. It's as abundant as the latter, but totally nocturnal and largely arboreal. This is a splendid mammal, unique and mysterious, and I was determined to know and photograph it. As Thornton Wilder writes, "[W]e can only be said to be alive in those moments when our hearts are conscious of our treasures."

Nothing stays the same! Everything is in flux! Life is a river, and you may dream you are an unmovable rock, but time and the flow will wear you away till you are pebble and sand. Count on it! The cabin that my cousin and I built collapsed one winter with the weight of the snow. So I decided to construct a home nearby and move back to paradise. And it was here, on the edge of the primeval forest, that I finally photographed the fifth squirrel.

Northern Flying Squirrel

I built a large freestanding bird feeder between the house and the forest, and finally I came to know something of these secretive squirrels. Their actions are incredibly quick and agile, and it was common to have half a dozen in the feeder at one time, all moving like members of Cirque du Soleil. Unlike the red squirrel who is a cantankerous loner, the flying squirrel is communal. As many as 50 have been found cuddling by gender for warmth in tree cavities or bird boxes although the number is normally less than six. They also share their food gathering areas.

All this night activity at my "bird" feeder invited predators. On several mornings, I found pieces of flying squirrel tail and fur lying on top of the snow. Who was coming to dinner? At night, I searched the surrounding forest with a strong lantern until I discovered a barred owl surveying his dinner menu. As I had caused this problem by enticing these squirrels to a large food cache, it was my responsibility to solve it. So, on top of the feeder I constructed a roof under which the owl could not fly. That solved the problem, so the barred owl returned to eating the many mice that gathered below the feeder to collect any fallen seeds.

Flying squirrels and owls are ancient adversaries, and each has helped to hone the other to perfection in its particular ecological niche. This clash is the forest version of an arms race; biologists call it coevolution by natural selection when two species evolve together, like wolves and deer, hummingbirds and certain flowers, bumblebees and the flowers they pollinate.

I also fed deer by dumping a bag of feed directly onto my driveway. Deer food is a nutritious mixture of corn, oats, and molasses. And when my driveway was plowed, a portion of this mixture was scattered through a snowdrift under a white pine tree. At least one inventive flying squirrel avoided my bird feeder entirely and collected kernels of corn while digging in this snowdrift under the safety of the pine tree. *See* photograph.

Eating Kernels of Corn

Because flying squirrels are neither hibernators like wood-chucks nor dormant like chipmunks, they must store food for winter's lean months. These larders are usually crammed with pinecones and fungi. I first became aware of this trait when I discovered one of my large nesting boxes stuffed with dried mushrooms.

Earlier that spring in a nearby bird box a flying squirrel had constructed a nest and was soon to give birth. Unaware of this, I opened the box surprising both of us. She jumped easily to the nearest tree where I took her photograph. Moments later she was back in *her* maternity box.

Expectant Mother

In early May, she had three babies in this bird box born blind, deaf, and hairless just like the baby red squirrels my cousin and I had found in the horse barn many years ago. They were so small, so vulnerable, as if still in their mother's womb. Nevertheless, after nursing on mother's milk for three months, they were ready to glide. Born helpless, dying helpless is the condition of all life. Ah, but the time between is wondrous. As they matured, a fur-covered membrane developed from their wrist to their ankles. With this and following their mother's example, these young flying squirrels step off the high branch into nothingness, and then, and then, they feel the wind beneath their wings, and all life's great potential before them.

First Flight

Though I am old with wandering
Through hollow lands and hilly lands,
I will find out where she has gone,
. . . .
And walk among long dappled grass,
And pluck till time and times are done,
The silver apples of the moon,
The golden apples of the sun.
William Butler Yeats, "The Song of Wandering Aengus"

CHAPTER—14

INSECTIA

I see trees of green, red roses, too,
I see them bloom, for me and you
And I think to myself
*What a wonderful world.**

His rough hands cupped the bumblebee in darkness, as we held our breath waiting for him to be stung. Seconds, perhaps a minute passed until, finally, my uncle opened his hands and let the bee fly free. "They're slow to sting, unlike hornets," he said. From that moment, my cousin and I were never afraid of bumblebees, nor were we ever stung. Apparently, bumblebees use their stinger as a last resort, although unlike many honeybees, wasps, and hornets, they can sting multiple times.

Bumblebee on My Grandmother's Honeysuckle

---

* Bob Thiele and George David Weiss, "What a Wonderful World," recorded in 1968 by Louis Armstrong.

Queen Bumblebee

The first thing I met was a bee with a buzz. Every spring, queen bumblebees fly erratically over the fields in search of an abandoned mouse nest. All early spring bees are queens, large and vigorous. These are the true wild bees of the Americas, not the puny domesticated honeybees from Europe. The rodent's nest with its abundant insulation will provide an ideal site for her to reestablish her lost colony of the previous summer. She's the previous year's sole survivor (unlike honeybees), and her eggs—fertilized last fall by short-lived drones—will produce new workers and a few late-summer drones (from unfertilized eggs). The poor drone, one brief summer fling and then he dies; any of his brothers still in the nest will be driven out to perish.

Within the mouse nest, the queen builds a wax honeypot and provisions it with nectar from early-blooming flowers. Next, she collects pollen and forms it into a mound on the floor of her nest. Here she will lay her eggs in the pile of pollen and coat them with wax secreted from her body. By shivering, the queen seeks to warm herself sufficiently to incubate her eggs—yes, some insects can change their body temperature. She is just like a mother hen on a clutch of eggs. For nourishment, she consumes honey from her wax pot, positioned within reach. In four days, the eggs, all of which will become female workers, hatch. The bumblebee queen continues her maternal care, foraging for pollen and nectar to feed to her larvae until they pupate. After this first brood emerges as adult bumblebees, the queen concentrates her efforts on laying eggs. Female worker bees raise the larvae and the colony numbers swell. At the end of summer, new queens and males are produced in order to create different colonies next year. After the new queens mate and become fertilized, the males all die, along with the female worker bees. The queens then seek shelter for the winter.

The summer after the red squirrel raised a family in the horse barn, bumblebees renovated her deserted grass nest. My cousin and I would climb the ladder to the barn's upper floor and watch the worker bees arrive laden with pollen balls on their hindmost legs (*see* "Bumblebee on My Grandmother's Honeysuckle"). If their activity slowed or stopped, we became impatient and would hit the log with a stick. Instantly a squadron of fighters would stream from the log, buzz about and then retire without firing a shot. Almost without exception, the workers had pollen balls when they arrived. But where did they store their gathered honey? It was many years before I learned they have a honey sac in their abdomens for just that purpose.

Bumblebee on Aster

Bumblebees and moths are the forgotten pollinators of the Americas. They go to every possible nectar source, not just the huge monoculture crops of modern farming, as honeybees tend to do. When European honeybees increase in an area, bumblebees decline and certain flowers remain unfertilized and eventually vanish.

Flowers and bumblebees have been dancing together for at least 100 million years. Presently, each needs the other to exist. It's noteworthy that different plants and trees bloom throughout the year so that the bees never starve and the blossoms are always pollinated: pussy willows and lilac in the spring, basswood trees in summer, and asters and goldenrod in the fall, to name a few. They have had time and generations to develop just such a wondrous relationship. Did the bees and trees think up this arrangement? Of course not! But the Blind Watchmaker did.

Black-Eyed Susan: Our View (left),
Bumblebee's View (right)
Photograph courtesy of *Wikipedia*

Our grandmother planted flowers on the south and west walls of the house with two staircases. My cousin and I would often go there to watch for the different pollinators to arrive. Ever observant, he commented on how few bumblebees went to the white compared to the blue flowers. Often half a dozen would be on the dark blue monkshood but none on the white petunias. "I wonder why that is," he added. Much later, I learned the answer to his question: bumblebees can see into the ultraviolet part of the light spectrum (red, orange, yellow, green, blue, indigo, violet, and *ultraviolet*). More incredibly, they were seeing a world entirely different than humans do. Consider the common black-eyed Susan (*see* photo) with its 13 Fibonacci petals. The photograph on the left is how we see the black-eyed Susan; the one on the right is how the same flower looks to bumblebees. It's a target of runway lights directing them to the nectar and pollen. There are more things in heaven and earth than dreamt of in the minds of two back-country boys.

My cousin and I were in a constant state of war with hornets and wasps. The war began when our cows wandered through a break in the fence onto the adjacent farm. We found them at the far end of this property, and almost at that moment one of them stepped into a hole with a bald-faced hornets' nest. As I recall, both beasts and boys were stung severely—but the trip home was quick, very quick.

By late August, the number of yellow jackets had increased dramatically, and we took great delight in destroying them. The gutter of the road by the house had sandbanks where some eastern yellow-jacket wasps dug holes for nests. This was a call to battle for us. We put on our shoes—a rare event—and picked up two wooden shingles fallen from the roof of the woodshed and a long thin stick. Arriving at the sandbank, we collected a small stone for a plug. First, we poked the stick into the nest until one or two wasps exited, then we quickly plugged the hole with the rock. Next, we hit them with our wooden shingles before stomping on them vigorously with our shoes. The routine was simple: unplug, agitate, plug, swat, and finally stomp. Tom Sawyer had less fun bamboozling his friends into whitewashing Aunt Polly's fence.

Some two decades ago, I returned alone to this happy place to find just weeds and wire bush. The barns were gone, and fields of wild raspberry canes now hold court where the barns once stood. No one would know humans had lived here unless they looked closely. I searched for signs of past life and found few: a large tree, the stone pond (now filled in), and the concrete cap on the well with the date September 1939. I saw little else until I looked even more closely.

Monkshood Blossom

The monkshood had escaped the confines of my grandmother's flower bed and was marching across the field down to the road. The bumblebees followed. In fact, bumblebees are this flower's only pollinator, for these blossoms (*see* photo) are too complex for honeybees and others to navigate. I think our grandmother would be pleased at this proliferation of her flowers, in spite of her unfulfilled need for neatness.

Now that I photograph the life around me, I have acquired an appreciation for the beauty of wasps and hornets.[*] Evolution has fashioned them both glorious and wonderful. Dylan Thomas thought otherwise. Remembering humorously in *A Child's Christmas in Wales*, he writes of the "Useful Presents" he received: "pictureless books . . . and books that told me everything about the wasp, except why." But science answers the question *how* not *why*. The *why question* is always personal and parochial while the *how answer* is non-personal and universal. When you fully understand the how of any aspect of life, that's enough. Science does not justify the ways of wasps to man. Bumblebees, wasps, and hornets exist for themselves, and that's enough!

Wasps: "forms most beautiful and most wonderful"

---

[*] Wasps have black and yellow rings, while hornets have black and white rings. Also, hornets are larger.

After a long summer's day of pollinating, the bumblebees, wasps, and hornets rest. And with evening's cool darkness, the night pollinators emerge from hiding by the millions. Although some plants and blossoms close when the sun goes down, others open, and these are the responsibility of the night pollinators. I mean those dull, brown moths that may annoy and tickle your face but mercifully do not bite. On a dark summer evening while returning from the barn on some errand or other, we would see them congregate on the amber glow from the windows. As boys, we had no interest in them, but my mother felt otherwise. She had a cedar chest for clothing she valued. Apparently, the smell of cedar confuses cloth-eating moth larvae, of which there are only two species.

Bruce Spanworm

Only after my cabin imploded and I built a permanent home on the back 40, did my negative attitude toward moths change. It was November and snow had already fallen and enticed me outside to check for fresh animal tracks. I was surprised to see a moth walking on the snow. A little research revealed this creature had the unattractive name of Bruce spanworm or "winter moth."

As the moth-eating birds had migrated south, these special fellows were safe to reproduce. William Butler Yeats mentions them in his poem "Song of the Wandering Aengus":

And when white moths were on the wing,
And moth-like stars were flickering out . . .

That was the day I had an attitude adjustment with respect to moths. Indeed, shortly after this, I went snowshoeing in search of moths, and, incredibly, I found several. Moths overwinter in all stages of their lifecycle: eggs, caterpillars, cocoons, and adults. And all forms can be found *even* in the coldest months.

Two Promethea Moth Cocoons

On my very first search for moths in winter, I photographed two Promethea moth cocoons hanging in cherry trees (pictured here), and a third I brought home and hung in my screened-in porch. Remarkably, in previous decades of wandering through these same fields with my cousin or alone, I had never noticed any cocoons. Granted they're wrapped in a leaf for camouflage from hungry birds and mice, but was I blind? Thoreau comments on this kind of blindness in the last paragraph of *Walden*:

> The light which puts out our eyes is darkness to us.
> Only that day dawns to which we are awake.
> There is more day to dawn.

I had been snowshoeing in the field by my grandfather's old barn, the one being swallowed by the forest, when I *first saw* the cocoons. Nature is inexorably reclaiming these fields. Initially, the low bush blackberries and wisteria took possession of the land; next, the cherry trees appeared from seeds passed through the bowels of birds and bears. In mast years, these trees are alive with such animals. Everyone is gone now, so the field is left to these cocoons, the stillness, and me.

Mating Promethea: Female (left), Male (right)

On the summer solstice, a female Promethea moth emerged from the cocoon on my screened-in porch releasing pheromones as she did so. Within an hour, six dark males appeared on the outside of the screen urgent to mate. I had *never seen* large black moths before and certainly not at 4 o'clock in the afternoon. Not being prudish, I carried the female still clinging to the cocoon to one of the eager males even though her wings were neither dry nor fully extended. They locked abdomens for what seemed a

long time while the unlucky suitors hovered nearby. The eggs must already have been in her abdomen when she emerged from the cocoon, ready for the male to fertilize them. Shortly after the nuptials, she laid the 10 eggs pictured here.

The name of this moth derives from the Greek hero Prometheus, the bringer of fire to humankind. Fittingly the female moth is flame colored while the male is burnt black.

The caterpillars that hatched from these eggs are incredible creatures appearing to be totally

Promethea Eggs

Adult Female and Adult Male Promethea

unrelated to the adult they will become (*see* respective photos). These green giants eat all summer, growing almost to the size of your forefinger before cocooning in the fall. After this, they never eat again because the mouth parts of adults are atrophied, like the eyes of cave fish. Their winter months are spent dangling from a twig wrapped in a leaf that offers no warmth. Although frozen, they will issue forth like the genie in Aladdin's lamp—a wondrous metamorphosis the next spring. As adults, they have one mission in life and only a few days to succeed: go forth and multiply. For the pair pictured here, it was mission accomplished. They died shortly afterward.

When you have procreated or when you are no longer able to—even with Viagra©—natural selection has no need of you.

Promethea Caterpillar

In Africa, whether on the hunt or on safari, guides speak of the big five: the lion, elephant, leopard, Cape buffalo, and rhinoceros. These mammals are unquestionably extraordinary. Nevertheless, *size alone should not* determine worth, lest we value nickels over dimes. Other criteria are beauty, color, form, and detail. In this respect, Ontario has its own big five, and they are all large insects: the giant silk moths. We have already seen one, the Promethea, and the other four, like the planets, are also named from characters in ancient mythology. See the chart for a list of these fabulous products from the Blind Watchmaker's hand.

Giant Silk Moths on the Farm		
Name	Wingspan	Caterpillar
Cecropia	11–15 cm	10 cm
Polyphemus	10–15 cm	7 cm
Promethea	8–10 cm	5 cm
Luna	8–10 cm	7 cm
Io	5–8 cm	7 cm

My cousin and I would have been entranced if we had found any of the Ontario "big five." Infrequently, we would discover a large tomato caterpillar, but we had no idea it would transform into an attractive hawk moth. As boys, however, we frequently

Cecropia Caterpillar

stumbled across one or another of the incredible caterpillars of the big five. They are intimidating creatures with red, blue, and yellow pegs (tubercles) and often hairs defensively protruding up and down their plump bodies. We had no notion what they might turn into—something worse we suspected, but no one could tell us.

As imposing as the Promethea caterpillar is with its four red pegs on the head and one yellow on its rear, the Cecropia larva is twice as long and is truly something to behold (*see* photos). Because of its size, colors, and numerous legs, some playfully refer to it as a 32 wheeler.

The Cecropia Head   Parasitoid Eggs

The reader might assume, as my cousin and I did, that anything this imposing was without enemies, but you would be wrong. These green sausages are a favorite food of the black-billed cuckoo, a great consumer of caterpillars. As well as enemies from above, caterpillars have even greater enemies from below. Various wasps and flies lay eggs either in or on the caterpillar; then these eggs hatch to larvae, which consume it from the inside. To compound this nightmare, these larvae eat the less vital parts first, so the caterpillar will live longer and stretch out the length of their dining for days. As Darwin writes, "I cannot persuade myself that a beneficent and omnipotent God would have designedly created the *Ichneumonidæ* [parasitic wasps] with the express intention of their feeding within the living bodies of caterpillars."

In the photograph showing the parasitoid eggs of the tachinid fly, the small black area to the right of each egg indicates it has hatched and the maggot has entered the body of this unfortunate caterpillar. The picture on the left shows two unhatched eggs between and slightly above two red pegs. It's gratifying to know that the tachinid fly itself has parasites, and they, in turn, are parasitic hosts as well.

This constant battle for existence is summed up by the English logician Augustus De Morgan in the following ditty:

> *Great fleas have little fleas*
> *upon their backs to bite 'em,*
> *And little fleas have lesser fleas,*
> *and so ad infinitum.*
> *And the great fleas themselves,*
> *in turn, have greater fleas to go on;*
> *While these again have greater still,*
> *and greater still, and so on.*

This is the condition of all life; It is what Shelley means in "Ode to the West Wind," when he writes, *"I fall upon the thorns of life! I bleed!"*

If by chance the Cecropia caterpillar avoids these ravaging flies and wasps, it will pupate. The cocoon is so large it doesn't

Cecropia Cocoon

hang from a twig but is attached lengthwise to a branch (*see* photo). Note the faint indication of an exit hole at the top of the cocoon. For extra protection from predators, the Cecropia builds a cocoon within a cocoon. Nevertheless, cocoons are vulnerable. A blue jay dropped an *opened* cocoon almost on the Red Spot directly in front of me. This bird, with some energy I'm certain, forced its way through both tough silk structures and devoured the pupa for its efforts.

If the caterpillar pupates with the maggots still devouring its innards, then they all die together.

Cecropia Male with 15 cm (6 inch) Wingspan

The farm has at least 2,000 species of moth; worldwide there are some 160,000. Butterflies, in comparison, have only a tenth of this number of species. The photograph of the Cecropia with the wingspan of 10 cm emphasizes its size, just one of its many attributes. The picture of its undercarriage displays its neon colors, red velvet stockings, and flawlessly formed antennae. Males have relatively larger antennae than females to more easily detect female pheromones (perfume) on the darkest of nights. Recent discoveries prove some moths see color even on a moonless night when humans see only shades of grey. What a piece of work is a Cecropia!

The Undercarriage of the Cecropia

Luna Moth

With the benefit of deep time and innumerable generations, evolution has abandoned few survival strategies. The Luna moth has gathered many of these. It seems an unlikely creation, translucent and delicate, almost a green leaf in the breeze. Often it mistakes a porch light for the moon from which it was named. It's a poor flyer, flapping about with difficulty to become airborne dragging a long, cumbersome tail. But this tail confuses the echolocation system of bats, its main predator, and the moth will gladly sacrifice its tail to save its life.

In the previous chapter, we explored the curious stratagem of countershading—that an animal with a white belly and a darker back appears flat or empty and therefore of no food value. Among those well able to defend themselves, such as skunks and porcupines, nature reverses countershading, producing a startling display to warn off experienced predators. With both adaptations in mind, we find the shading of the helpless Luna caterpillar (*see* photo) paradoxical because its belly is darker than its back, so it's shaded like a

Luna Larva

skunk. This larva, however, habitually lives *upside down*, making it perfectly countershaded for camouflage. Nature is full of surprises.

We're going fishing! Right after a breakfast of eggs, potatoes, biscuits, and milk, my cousin and I leave the house with the two staircases and turn north to walk to Brady Lake, some 6 miles (10 km) away. We have no rods or reels, just a Players Flat Fifty cigarette tin to hold our few hooks, sinkers, and line. Along the way, we drink at a spring and pick berries for lunch. Midway in our journey, we come to the causeway of slab wood resting on a swampy floor. Fortunately, this causeway is now high above the water but still alive with water snakes and turtles. When we get close to the lake, we break off two long tag alder branches for our fishing rods. But since the alders are alive, they don't break cleanly so my cousin uses his ever-ready pen knife to finish the job. He loves his pen knives, especially the ones with colored handles. This one is new with a beautiful blue inlay.

My mother and father left the mill only five years ago, yet it's gone, dismantled and sold. The Boyd House, however, is still in good condition with new tenants, although the cookhouse has been demolished. In the early days of lumbering, sawdust and slab wood were discarded. The former created a large hill; the latter, piled at the lakeside, collapsed into the water to form a vast labyrinth of tunnels and caves between slimy-green boards. Here bullhead catfish live in their thousands.

We locate an old rowboat with a bailing can and row to the catfish labyrinth. It's eerie watching schools of black catfish exit the maze and rise to our hook, baited with a piece of our grandmother's red yarn. Quickly we catch two dozen. Then either his line or mine becomes hooked on one of the boards. So out comes the blue-handled pen knife to snip the line. Reaching over the boat to make the cut close to the water's surface, the knife slips through his wet fingers. I see its slow spiral descent into the tea-brown labyrinth as it disappears forever between the slabs.

Without our usual enthusiasm, we catch more catfish, 47 in all. After, we return the rowboat, bailing all the while; then we sit quietly in the sun on the remains of the mill's long pier, continuing to fish. My cousin catches three large bass; I catch two. We walk home satisfied and happy.

My aunt makes us clean all the fish, which she cooks immediately. All the fish are eaten that night for dinner; they feed our grandmother, my aunt and uncle, my cousin's two sisters, and the fishermen. We are proud providers.

Pumpkinseed Sunfish

I still remember the sights, sounds, and smells of that day. But most of all, when I recollect that idyll, I vividly recall the blue-handled pen knife spiraling to its eternal resting place in the tea-brown labyrinth and the surface of that murky water sparkling in the sunshine as we sat on the warm pier. Our mood improved—the sun was young.

Not long after, we each caught a pumpkinseed sunfish, a small creature of consummate beauty (*see* photo). After a detailed inspection, we released our beauties into their weedy garden. This humble fish with its exquisite spots elevated our spirits to Christmas-morning levels, for we were in love with color and life. Behind each eye was a large, curious spot, which we wondered about, but bigger fish interpret as an eye to be reckoned with. Biologists call this *eyespot mimicry*.

Eyespot mimicry is common in moths, butterflies, birds, mammals, and, as we have seen, fish. Clearly, their main purpose is to postpone dinner for some larger predator or draw attention away from a vulnerable body part. The Promethea, Luna, and Cecropia have relatively small eyespots compared to the Io moth, who seems to have pulled out all the stops for eyespots (*see* photo). Invert the picture of the Io moth to point its

Io Moth, Head Down

head upward, and note that the impact of the mimicry is lessened because the abdomen no longer plays the role of a nose. Moths have forewings and hind wings, and, when these moths are resting, the former cover the latter. In the case of the Io moth, the large eyes are on the hind wings, ready to flash and startle any would-be predator. Although they are the smallest of the big five, they are also the most abundant.

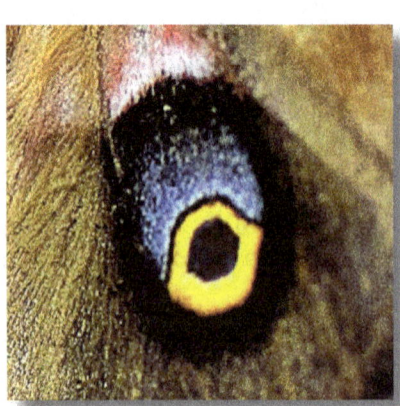

Eye of the Cyclops

My favorite among the big five is the Polyphemus moth, named for the Cyclops Odysseus blinded. It's as large as your outstretched hand, and its eye mimicry is the best of any creature in the Americas. This moth defensively flashes its underwings to show the eyespots (*see* photos), and to avoid the "stare effect" it *shivers* them.

Male Polyphemus Moth

They are puny creatures! They are parasites devouring the trees and shrubs of the third planet of an ordinary star, one of 300 billion, in a small arm of an out-of-the-way spiral galaxy, a minor part of the Local Group of galaxies, a minute fraction of the Virgo Supercluster, one of innumerable such clusters, a minute part of the mighty Laniakea—a mote in the eye of the universe. Yet, they are fashioned as if from the mind of Leonardo or Michelangelo, painted with the entire splendor a Renaissance brush can afford. They are splendid creatures!—rolled out of stardust, baked in the furnace of broken symmetry, crafted over eons in the workshop of the Blind Watchmaker. What a piece of work is a moth!

Insects first appeared on earth about 480 million years ago, long before reptiles, birds, mammals, and man. Their various forms account for three quarters of all life. Whether the world ends in fire or in ice, insects will still be here—and not just the ubiquitous cockroach scuttling out from under a nuclear reactor. Many insects, such as the common fruit fly, are radiation resistant, even more resistant than cockroaches. Smaller organisms do even better. Water bears or tardigrades (slow walkers) can survive the vacuum of space, boiling water, and just about absolute zero, and they were here millions of years before insects. They have survived all of the "big five" mass extinctions over the last half billion years. Tardigrades (*see* photo) are everywhere on earth. They live in moss, lichen, leaf litter, and soil; they live in fresh or salt water.

Fully grown they are about a millimeter long, the size of the period at the end of this sentence, just visible to the human eye. Russian cosmonauts have found *live* tardigrades on the *outside* of the International Space Station—no cogent explanation has been forthcoming as to how they got there. Be humble in the presence of such incredible adaptation.

Water Bear or Tardigrade courtesy of Google

I see skies of blue and clouds of white,
The bright blessed day, the dark sacred night
And I think to myself
What a wonderful world.

Yes, I think to myself
What a wonderful world

CHAPTER—15

THE WARRIOR CLASS

In the sun born over and over,
I ran my heedless ways,

. . . .

Before the children green and golden
Follow him out of grace. . .
Dylan Thomas, "Fern Hill"

In our endless pursuit of all things living and beautiful, we were destined to discover something rare and unique. Early one morning, my cousin and I walked back of the "new" barn directly into an area called the "slash." Here our grandfather, and then my uncle, had a sugar shack with a small evaporator to make maple syrup. These woods were relatively open with the odd apple tree set in the midst of a grove of old sugar maples.

Not far into this peaceful wood, a large, fur-covered creature jumped out of a maple tree directly in front of us. In my memory, it paused momentarily when it hit the earth, turned its head, and looked directly at us. Astonished, yet unafraid, we stood our ground, and the creature ran off toward the forest, dark and deep—an experience never to be forgotten.

A Fisher in Fall

No one seemed to know what it was. Some thought we were inventing tall tales, but we knew what we had seen. It was as if we had met a giant with a friend named Jack who tried to sell us a handful of magic beans. Looking back, the reaction of the adults seems hypocritical, for they themselves were fond of their own fantastic stories: snakes that cured goiters, alligator-sized lizards in the swamps, and immense man-eating wolves and bears. Thereafter, we kept such experiences to ourselves.

Decades passed, and this handsome mammal with its golden-brown coat became common again, as it had been in the distant past, before almost trapped to extinction. What we had seen was the legendary fisher (*see* photos); males are 4 feet (120 cm) of muscle and sinew with the appearance of a small bear, but twice as feisty. They are absolutely fearless!

What does a fisher eat? Well, pretty much whatever it wants. But contrary to popular belief, fishers do not hunt or eat fish or, for that matter, even like water. The large male in the photograph was checking out a woodchuck hole for a possible meal. Fishers prey on birds and small mammals, including snowshoe hares, mice, squirrels, and porcupines, which they vanquish by attacking the only quill-free spot on a porcupine's body—the face. In this case, reverse countershading helps the fisher find the porcupine. I once found the carcass of a wild turkey under a roosting tree. As mentioned in Chapter 3, "Turkey Shoot," tom turkeys fly to the very top of white pine trees in winter, enduring extreme cold but generally escaping fishers, who are excellent climbers.

Large Male Fisher in Summer

In my unending attempt to know this place for the first time, I have taken a quarter of a million photographs and videos of all things bright and beautiful. My cousin and I started this boyhood mission when the earth was young and green. Photographs from my camera traps, like the ones of Mother Courage, account for many of these and most of the videos.

Young Fisher in Spring

I print some of the best photographs to share with friends. Inevitably, when I show them a picture of a fisher, they first ask, "Aren't they extremely vicious?" To which I reply, "They are as vicious as they need to be to survive." The consistency of their question elevates it to the status of a *meme*, (rhymes with *gene*). As an attempt to explain the way cultural information spreads, Richard Dawkins introduces the idea of the meme and coins the word in his marvelous book *The Selfish Gene*. The meme is to culture as the gene is to biology. For example, young men sometimes wear their baseball caps backwards to indicate heightened testosterone levels (I'm being polite). By extension, the concept has evolved to include, for example, videos, graphics, and slogans passed on digitally over social media.

Now I grant you the picture of the "Large Male Fisher in Summer" may give anyone pause, but the "Young Fisher in the Spring" is delightful. One size, or one remark, does not fit all; when a remark is offered regardless of fit, it's a meme.

Fishers are members of the weasel family who generally have a bad reputation. Not long ago a YouTube meme of the African honey badger as a totally badass animal was making the rounds through social media—it was on the evening news. The fisher has unfortunately fallen to that level in North America. To counter this perception, I again present another cute and curious fisher from deep in the winter forest.

Young Fisher in Winter

Although I regularly photograph fishers in all seasons with my camera traps, it is always a special event to see a live one. A meeting with a fisher, rising to the level of the encounter my cousin and I had with one in the slash, occurred on a cold winter night. About 2:00 am, I was awakened by a loud noise at my bedroom window. Investigating with my flashlight, I was astounded to see a very large fisher standing on its hind legs splat against the window glass. His eyes gleamed with the light as I went closer, inches closer, and we looked at each other and neither was afraid, but both were spellbound. Two aliens evolutionarily separated by at least 200 million years scanned one another. Clearly, I wasn't the only one who wanted to know this place for the first time.

After what seemed some minutes, he jumped to the snow-covered ground in the moonlight and disappeared into the eternal green forest behind my home. That night, two predators took the measure of each other.

Fisher at Sunset Disappearing into the Forest

The pine marten (*see* photo), at one-fifth the weight, is a miniature version of the fisher. More northern and more arboreal than its larger relative, it inhabits the earth's entire circumpolar region. The farm is at the marten's southern limit, and my cousin and I never saw or even heard of one. Similar to the fisher, martens were over-hunted in the past. Since those early days, I have seen two, but my camera traps have photographed many, and they have even yielded a few videos[*]. In Russia, martens are called sable and valued for their rich golden fur. Like all members of the weasel family, they are fierce carnivores of flying squirrels, chipmunks, mice, voles, and so on, and regularly kill animals several times their own size. As with the fisher, they are fearless, the Spartans of the animal world. They give no quarter and expect none!

Pine Marten

[*] Google "pine marten and flying squirrel" for my YouTube video.

The mustelids, the family of carnivorous mammals to which the martens belong, are the warrior class of the mammal world. They form a diverse group, fill numerous ecological niches, have ingenious evolutionary adaptations, and include wolverines, fishers, pine martens, mink, river otters, ermines, and weasels. Evolution has been busy here over millions of years. Wolverines can crack a moose femur to get at the marrow. Fishers regularly kill and eat porcupines. Pine martens readily run down red squirrels in trees. Mink are semiaquatic to increase their food base, as are river otters. And ermine grow a white coat for winter camouflage, and, because of their shape and size, they can pursue prey into its burrow. I once saw a relentless and fearless mink kill a snowshoe hare by severing its spinal column. Initially, I thought to help the hare, but it had already suffered a paralyzing injury. Helpless, I let nature run its course.

The farm had three outhouses, other than the great outdoors. One was attached to the side of the horse barn, another to the woodshed, and the last to the barn that later housed the pigeons. All three outhouses were two-seaters, and yes, that means exactly what you think it means. My cousin and I normally used the closest, the one attached to the woodshed. While we were enjoying the luxury of our gravity-fed water closet—with the door open—a weasel (*see* photo) joined us and vigorously pulled at

Short-tailed Weasel aka Ermine

my pant leg. Short-tailed weasels while not an everyday event were common. I shook my leg until it lost interest and disappeared through a crack in the boards into the woodshed. We gave chase through a door.

The interior had cords of split and piled maple, beech, and elm wood stacked neatly against winter's appalling cold, and a variety of axes and saws plus a large grindstone. On one particular pile, the weasel would appear and disappear at short intervals. We thought she probably had a nest with babies (kits), which we were determined to find.

Never was wood more quickly unstacked, but the weasel vanished. Because my cousin and I had some idea of how hard the adults worked, we restacked the wood. In all the decades since, I have had many encounters with weasels, but I have never found a nest of young weasel kits. Yet we did discover something almost as unexpected behind this woodpile—a large bottle of my father's homemade dandelion wine.

As boys, we tried to imitate adults. One August, we collected dried clover heads and rubbed them between our palms until something like tobacco appeared. This we rolled in my uncle's cigarette papers before lighting up back of the horse barn. It made us sick! And when we became adults, neither of us smoked. My mother and her sisters smoked when their husbands weren't around, trusting their children wouldn't tell on them. We never did.

Back to the homemade wine. To allay our sorrows over the vanished weasel, we tried the wine. It was awful, absolutely awful, but we drank it anyway for we were men! This was the wrong day, however, to test our manhood, because later that afternoon we were to walk to the original farm to have supper with my mother's only brother and his wife, the lady with the goiter. It was some distance as the two farm houses were on opposite ends of their respective 100 acres. Off we went with my grandmother, my aunt and uncle, and my cousin's two sisters. Now cow paths are thin and difficult to navigate when sober, but a real test when not. I recall someone holding my hand as I staggered through the fields. After throwing up in the great outdoors, I felt better but neither my cousin nor I could eat our supper.

Ermine

He sat slumped in a corner like a bag of potatoes while I lay on a small couch, trying to stop the world from spinning. His sisters laughed at us, but the adults gave us no reprimands. In the future, however, I never drank to that degree again, but my cousin needed more lessons.

In winter, the short-tailed weasel transforms into the legendary ermine (pictured here) prized for its fur. Incredibly, furriers require at least 150 ermine pelts to make just one full-length coat—so much death with so little meaning.

Their curiosity and fearlessness are not lost with a change of clothes. I have had them run out of rock piles or from under old buildings in winter and circle around my feet as if to bite my pant leg in remembrance of another age. To intimidate, they look you directly in the eye, and, despite my size, in their mind I could be a meal.

Consider one of the great paintings of the Renaissance, Leonardo's *The Lady with an Ermine*. As with most of da Vinci's works, this portrait has been much overpainted and "restored" in the 500 years or so since its creation, but the head of the girl, her hand, and the arresting presence of the ermine are surely the master's own. What do they tell us? What do they say after five centuries?

Leonardo is comparing the lady to the ermine, the human to the animal. She was Cecilia Gallerani, the 16-year-old mistress of Ludovico Sforza, ruler of Milan, and patron to da Vinci. It was for Sforza Leonardo painted *The Last Supper*. The ermine, called a

Lady with an Ermine

stoat in Europe, was the heraldic symbol of purity and the adopted emblem of the Sforza family. The artist was suggesting a comic parallel between her lack of purity and the figurative chasteness of the beast. It seems likely Leonardo viewed her with some caution because of her scheming ways.

As Jacob Bronowski writes in *Science and Human Values*, the whole picture is in some sense a pun. Leonardo has matched the ermine to the maid. Her body is turned in the opposite direction to her head, as is the stoat's; all eyes are fixed on something off canvas. Her claw-like hand strokes the beast's back, and its paw seems to do the same to her arm. The flattened hair emphasizes her wide forehead, which is like that of the animal. I believe this ermine is one of the most perfectly painted animals of the Renaissance: the sinuousness of its body, the power of its gaze, and the arresting perfection of its head are matchless. The beautiful head of the girl contrasts with the tightness of her lips and the slight upward curl of her mouth, which lends her an air of limited mental ability. Bronowski catches the parallel and states the pattern:

> As we look, the emblematic likeness springs as freshly in our minds as it did in Leonardo's when he looked at the girl and asked her to turn her head. *The Lady with a Stoat* [an ermine] is as much a research into man and animal, and a creation of unity, as is *Darwin's Origin of Species*.[*]

The cautious reader may think I'm finding meanings and making inferences from Leonardo's masterpiece that the artist never intended. With Leonardo, this is never the case. From his art notebooks, we know how much thought he put into the presentation of his subject.

Weasels have the classic profile of a small predator: short legs and a long thin body. They also have a badass disposition. The mongoose is similarly built for a similar ecological niche. This is another example of convergent evolution, which we explored previously by considering the woodchuck and the wombat or the swallows and the

---

[*] Jacob Bronowski, *Science and Human Values* (New York: Harper & Row, 1972), p. 28.

swifts. Chimney swifts are often mistaken for swallows, but they are only distantly related; whereas tree and barn swallows are close. Animals in similar ecological niches look alike.

It's an illusion, however, that nature is molding life, whether weasel or mongoose, woodchuck or wombat, according to a fixed plan. That view is false, utterly false! Natural selection cares not for the future and knows nothing of the past. There is just the here and the now—this moment in time. A succession of present moments has molded members of the mustelids to be warriors as vicious as they need to be: strong and vigorous, quick and agile, and fearless beyond reason.

Fisher up a Tree

The very word "evolution" is misleading because it implies a direction, specifically an upward direction. Many dictionaries give an incorrect definition for it—even as their primary meaning. Somewhere they will say we're evolving upward from the simple to the complex. Yet sometimes organisms, especially parasites, adapt by becoming less complex: the classic example is the tapeworm, just a head with a segmented stomach.

The correct definition of evolution implies no road map, and the preferred phrase is the one Darwin often used, "descent with modification." The notion that evolution has a direction—and worse an overriding purpose—is outmoded and false. We are riders in a vast whirlwind of events over immense eras, forever adapting to the here and now or perishing. This is the condition of all organisms; it's the human condition, and we must deal with it.

All evolutionary outcomes are contingent on a multitude of quirks and accidents. It's possible, for example, that one early vertebrate worm was responsible for the evolution of all later vertebrates. Had some accident such as climatic change eliminated that worm, human beings would never have existed.

In his splendid book *Wonderful Life*, Stephen Jay Gould fully develops the concept of contingent history with numerous detailed examples from the Burgess Shale in the Canadian Rockies of British Columbia, Canada. The book's title comes from Frank Capra's famous Christmas movie *It's a Wonderful Life*— Hollywood's unsurpassed example of contingency.

In the final chapter of *Wonderful Life*, Gould imagines seven possible worlds as life might have been. Yet the combinations stirred by life's contingencies are such that he could as easily have imagined seven million.

We will let Gould speak for himself of the species closest to his heart and ours. The metaphor is a movie theater running the tape called "Life":

> Run the tape again, and let the tiny twig [on the bush] of *Homo sapiens* expire in Africa. Other hominids may have stood on the threshold of what we know as human possibilities, but many sensible scenarios would never generate our level of mentality. Run the tape again, and this time Neanderthal perishes in Europe and *Homo erectus* in Asia (as they did in our world). The sole surviving stock, *Homo erectus* in Africa, stumbles along for a while, even prospers, but does not speciate and therefore remains stable. A mutated virus then wipes *Homo erectus* out, or a change in climate reconverts Africa into inhospitable forest. One little twig on the mammalian branch, a lineage with interesting possibilities that were never realized, joins the vast majority of species in extinction. So what? Most possibilities are never realized, and who will ever know the difference?
>
> Arguments of this form lead me to the conclusion that biology's most profound insight into human nature, status, and potential lies in the simple phrase, the embodiment of contingency: *Homo sapiens* is an entity, not a tendency.

How are we to deal with this view of life and history emotionally? No design; no slime to man; no ultimate purpose; just endless, meaningless chance. Well we begin by recalling that Bertrand Russell thought happiness depends mostly on good digestion. And Gould wisely writes that contingent history gives us *maximum freedom* to thrive, each in our own individualistic way.

Pine Marten   Mink

Fisher   Weasel

THE WARRIOR CLASS

In my persistent ambling through forest and field, always finding something unexpected, I occasionally discover a dead weasel. These mustelids live fast, fight hard, and die young, males usually in the first year and females after three years, if they're lucky. While sauntering near the barn being swallowed by the forest, I always turn over the sheets of metal roofing scattered through the field. At the right time of day, not too hot nor too cold, I find abundant life: several different species of snake, mice, voles, shrews, ant colonies, and often the unforeseen.

On one dull, cool fall day, I wasn't expecting much, but the first sheet I lifted revealed a dead short-tailed weasel (pictured here). His body was preparing to put on the white coat of winter, and he to change his name to ermine. Surprised, I looked closer. Beside the deceased was a small mound of fine grass which

I removed, exposing an equally dead red-backed vole (the red is very faint, even in life). It seems the weasel had killed the vole and hidden it for a later meal. But the weasel lay down beside his larder for a nap that became an eternity. I have no way of knowing exactly how he died, but it was not of hunger, a trap, gun, poison, or another predator. Clearly, he had been one of the lucky ones; few warriors die on a soft bed in their sleep with abundant food by their side.

Death of a Short-Tailed Weasel

Wild weasel who caught and sang the sun in flight,
Do not rage against the dying of the light.
Go, go gentle into that good night.[*]

---

[*] My apologies to Dylan Thomas and his poem "Do Not Go Gentle into That Good Night."

CHAPTER—16

THE SKY GODS

And nightly under the simple stars
As I rode to sleep the owls were bearing the farm away,
All the moon long I heard, blessed among stables, the nightjars**
Flying with the ricks, and the horses
Flashing into the dark.
Dylan Thomas, "Fern Hill"

My mother told me a story that I will now tell you, the reader. I was in middle age when I heard it, but she was younger—Mother was young right up until she died. Her only brother was setting snares for hares, possibly for the meat, certainly for the fur. Snares strangle their luckless prey, and the more it struggles the tighter the wire around its neck becomes until all life drains away. While setting his traps, this hunting uncle chanced to see a great horned owl sitting in a tree; clearly it was after the same rabbits but during the night shift. The following day, my uncle took my mother, who was very much a tomboy, to see this glorious bird of prey. Now owls are creatures of habit for they will sit on the same branch of a tree year after year so that, once discovered, they are easily found a second time. Mother had an eye for beauty plus she told me how impressed she was with its size and bearing. That should have been the end of the story, but it wasn't.

Great Horned Owl

* Nightjars are the European equivalent of whip-poor-wills.

Within a few nights, as luck would have it, the owl itself was garroted in one of these snares, doubtless in pursuit of a hare. Perhaps out of a sense of guilt this uncle took the owl to a taxidermist to be stuffed and mounted as if still living.

After World War I, my mother's brother inherited the original farm, and my grandfather moved to the adjacent farm with its vast system of barns and the five-bedroom home with the two staircases. And he took the stuffed great horned owl with him. This is the owl that my cousin and I saw every night when we went to bed, the one at the top of one of the staircases. I would gently run my hand over his head momentarily flattening his two feathered ears before caressing his long broad back. To my mind, this great bird closed his eyes in pleasure, and as I lay down to dreams, he patrolled the silent fields. Where is he now I wonder?

Great Horned Owl Patrolling the Fields

I'm not certain how many species of owl live or migrate through the farm. My uncle thought there was only one, although my cousin and I often heard two distinctly different calls. The classic "*hoo-h'HOO-hoo-hoo*" of the great horned owl we somehow knew, yet a second and more persistent call echoed from the deep forest asking a question, "*Who cooks for you? Who cooks for you all?*" Years passed before I discovered, this second call was from a barred owl—a bird of the deep woods.

During any season, a walk to one of the barns at night was exciting. We would stand in the barnyard bathed by moonlight with bats coursing through the air, owls calling, wolves howling in the distance, foxes barking in the slash, the music of whip-poor-wills and nighthawks echoing—surely this was Eden.

Other than these familiar sounds, we also heard many calls we didn't know, and at least one of these calls was a third owl. These trips to the barn at night were often to attend a sick or injured animal or one about to give birth.

Frequently, while walking in the springtime, we would hear a repetitive metallic sound "*too-too-too*," clear and sharp, repeated endlessly. At that time, none of us realized this mechanical clanking was the love song of the exquisite, diminutive saw-whet owl (*see* photo), which is about the size of a robin. These owls are often heard but seldom seen and rarely photographed. In a lifetime, I have seen just three although they are common.

Northern Saw-Whet Owl

It was late November and, overnight, the first snow had fallen to the depth of a boy's fist. After breakfast, my cousin and I bolted from the house, like cows being released from the barn in the springtime. We were looking for animal tracks, any record of last night's activity. Through the barnyard and down the rough road we went toward the spring field. Before walking far, we saw the tracks of a red squirrel (they're H shaped) and of two deer (they're four large spots with drag marks). Encouraged and in high spirits, as was our dog, we continued. It wasn't long before we saw it. The spring field was open except for a few scattered crab apple trees where, two decades later, I came across the pine grosbeaks in a snowstorm. But today was sunny and as we turned the final corner and entered the field, we saw it sitting on an old fence post. I caught the dog lest he chase away this apparition of the high Arctic before we had a good look. The great

Snowy Owl

bird watched us for some minutes, as we stood transfixed in its presence. Then this phantom flew so silently on wings so large that he took our breath away. Gliding low over the fields, the snowy owl turned a curve and then, by god, he was gone except in our imaginations. I released the struggling dog, but he did not give chase. We kept knowledge of this apparition to ourselves for fear the adults would think we had met the giant with a friend named Jack again.

Snowy Owl Flying

In the years of a lemming die-off in the high Arctic, these owls erupt in large numbers to the south. Every three to five winters a diligent search of back roads will reveal one of these spectacular birds. Since that first snowy owl my cousin and I saw in the spring field, I have seen a dozen more.

Bird books tell us there are ten species of owl in Ontario; I have mentioned four of those found on the farm. The fifth is so rare that, in my life, I have seen only one (pictured here). It was early winter and I was walking with friends near my new home on the back 40 through a grove of cedar trees. Glancing near the top of a large tree, I chanced to see what looked like a miniature great horned owl, the one at the head of the stairs. Perhaps because they're a top predator, fear does not come readily to them. He watched us intently, but did not fly as we photographed him for some minutes. It was actually a long-eared owl, and he was among friends; we left him to daydream about whatever he wanted.

Long-Eared Owl

After there were no more cows on the farm, their paths through the fields quickly disappeared, and, with the eternal creep of the forest, the fields themselves finally vanished. Although the slash is little changed, the spring field is gone, completely gone. Because great horned owls prefer openness, they have also left. It has been two decades since I saw the last one at Walden Pond sitting atop a dead tree surveying for lunch. He saw me first and silently flew the length of the pond to another snag. I no longer hear their grand hooting in the evening, but the persistent *"Who cooks for you? Who cooks for you all?"* of the barred owl grows louder with each year. This land is now their land.

Vanished Warrior: Great Horned Owl

All owls are unique, but the barred owl is truly singular. It's the only owl in eastern North America with totally black eyes; plus it has a Shakespearean vocabulary for the bird world. Beyond its constant questioning of who is cooking for us, it produces an endless stream of shrieks, hisses, hoots, screeches, squawks, cackles, and chortles, and gives off an absolutely demonic laugh during courtship and mating. Because this owl has such an extensive vocabulary, which it uses in various combinations and modulations, we can easily see how those humans with supernatural tendencies could associate it with things that go bump in the night. Sound travels great distances in the forest; sight doesn't reach beyond the next tree, so these birds need a large lexicon to communicate.

Barred Owl Triptych

As my home on the back 40 was right on the edge of the primeval forest, I came to know these owls. They arrived most nights in the summer and, every night in the winter, sat on the same branch of an old maple tree. From this roost, the owl had a clear view of my large bird feeder and the surrounding area; red-backed voles, mice, rabbits, and flying squirrels were also regular night visitors to the Sunflower Seed Café. You might ask how I knew the owl was on its perch since it was nighttime; a quick survey with my flashlight revealed its presence.

Despite all this easy winter visibility, this bird is secretive, incredibly so when raising a family. Let me explain. Some decades past, Dutch elm disease spread through North America killing these majestic trees. At the northwest corner of my property was the largest tree on the farm, and it was an elm; this tree was so large three adults could just reach around it. It took years for the disease to kill the tree, but death was inevitable. First, it lost its huge branches, but it took another two decades before the trunk crashed to earth in a violent wind and rain storm.

While walking past this fallen trunk a few days later, my ever-curious dog discovered a cavity nest in the tree with the eggshells of a barred owl—pure, white, and spherical. Happily this was late August so the owlets had long since left the nest. This tree was within sight and sound of my home, with the road beside it. How did I miss finding this nest, probably reused for several years? My cousin and I prided ourselves on our ability to find bird nests; we'd found hundreds—recall we had an egg collection. I'm much older and more experienced now, but these years haven't enhanced my abilities at nest finding. On many a quiet night, I could hear the footfalls of the owls as they walked along the peak of my house. These raptors were hiding in plain sight, and I didn't find them!

Barred Owl: Voice of the Deep Forest

It's a truism that everything is in flux. Ecclesiastes 1:9, however, says, "There is no *new thing* under the sun," but it would be more accurate if it had said, "There is no *same thing* under the sun." The farm lost the great horned owl but gained both the wild turkey and the turkey vulture. Neither of these birds was here when my cousin and I roamed these fields.

Turkey vultures soar effortlessly in a shallow "V" with rarely a wing flap during a summer's afternoon. Their wingspan is beyond that of eagles, yet humans consider them the lowlifes of the avian world. If hot, they pee on their legs to cool off, and, if confronted, they vomit the foul contents of their stomachs, which is often more than enough to dissuade a predator. But worst of all, they regularly eat carrion, lots of carrion. Clearly, this creature is not your sweet hummingbird at a daffodil. They don't sing and they don't dance, but they can hiss and they can whine, and they take out the garbage all the time.

Wild Turkey versus Turkey Vulture: The New Guys

Because of the phenomenal abundance of food that modern agriculture has brought, we forget that, for 90 percent of human history, hunting and gathering was humanity's adaptation in the struggle for food. And "gathering" definitely included collecting carrion and large bones for meat and marrow respectively. Worse yet, history—both distant and recent—records numerous cases of human cannibalism. Predators such as eagles and wolves will not disdain a free meal of a dead deer—they dare not! It's with the carcasses of road-killed deer that I've gotten my photographs and videos of both these majestic animals.

I discovered the hypocrisy of human squeamishness about eating bodies, dead or alive, early on, when my cousin and I explored the deserted farms that were returning to forest. Even before my uncle abandoned the farm, others had already left; their homes were scattered all over this land. Beyond the slab causeway, my dad had a still in an empty house hidden from the road. When my cousin and I roamed this land like young foxes, there was a dilapidated house five or six farms south of ours. We enjoyed exploring these old buildings, once homes but now novel habitat for nature's creatures. All these houses were two-stories high because the heat from the woodstove in winter would rise and warm the second floor—at least that was the idea. This particular house had been abandoned for decades, and, as luck would have it, we discovered a large honeybee nest on the outside staircase wall. Without speaking, we each snatched a handful of the exposed honey-dripping comb, ran around the corner, and hid in the staircase. The bees never found us, as we greedily ate our honey and spit out the wax.

Just as I was about to take my last bite, I noticed the comb also contained bee larvae—we had been eating maggots with our honey but were none the worse. After all, they were protein. If we could eat maggots and not be squeamish, let's allow the vultures to eat carrion and not be judgmental. In our own small way, my cousin and I were hunter-gatherers.

A Vulture on the Remains of a Raccoon

Turkey vultures have one ability beyond that of every other bird—even their African cousins don't possess this skill. To test this talent, I picked up a freshly killed rabbit on the road; blood still trickled from its head after it lost an argument with a car. Arriving home, I carefully placed its still warm body under a large white pine tree so that it wasn't visible from the sky. The time was approximately 8:00 pm. At 7:00 am the following morning, two huge turkey vultures had found the rabbit's hidden body, and they must have done it by *smell* alone. With a vast green canopy covering the land, they use this method of finding carcasses. Look closely at the close-up of the turkey vulture and note that its nostrils go right through the beak to pick up as much scent as possible. On the African savannah without trees, vultures hunt by sight not scent. Though most birds have little or no sense of smell—great horned owls kill and eat skunks—vultures are the connoisseurs of odor.

A Vulture's Apartment

The derelict house (*see* "A Vulture's Apartment") was a home when my cousin and I were boys—we visited there many times. Because of hardship and time, the owners abandoned it to new tenants. The trees and shrubs took over the yard, porcupines rented the earthen basement, eastern phoebes nested on the walls of the main floor, and turkey vultures took over the attic. They entered their apartment through the top left window. Because

Soaring Turkey Vulture

these birds will desert a nest if disturbed, I only investigated when I was certain they had raised and fledged their "beautiful" babies. When I finally inspected the upstairs, there was no nest to speak of, just a depression in a pile of debris and an unbelievable stench. But this shelter had been enough for these strange birds to recycle the dead into the living. Few can claim as much!

My uncle's pride and joy was his Winchester lever-action 30/30 rifle that he hunted deer with in November. The other uncle, my mother's brother, had a .22 rifle he used to shoot at "chicken hawks." Now a "chicken hawk" was likely the red-tailed hawk, a chunky bird, mostly white breasted, with a fiery tail.

During a warm summer day, these hawks would make large lazy circles in the sky while scanning the fields for food. The sight of one gave my cousin and me a sense of freedom and power, and if the sun were in the right place in the sky, we could look up and see the deep russet red through their tails (*see* tail feather photo). This other uncle hated them, and his wife, the lady with the goiter, was equally agitated. At the sight of a hawk, any hawk, he would take his rifle, put in a .22 long cartridge, and shoot. He always missed, and my cousin and I had to stifle a laugh and quickly run away. The hawk also wisely departed to friendlier fields. To them all hawks were chicken killers; nonetheless, neither my cousin nor I ever saw a hawk attempt a kill.

Red-Tailed Hawk: A Sky God

Now according to this uncle and aunt, all snakes were poisonous, all hawks were hen killers, and all birds were pests. They were at war with the natural world, so my cousin and I didn't like them. We knew this uncle was cruel to his horses for he often hit them with a pitchfork, and he was no better to his other animals; worst of all, he left his dog outside even on brutally cold winter nights.

Once, I recall, my cousin's father asked this uncle to kill a pig—apparently he was an expert. Somehow, the pig became aware of his murderous intentions and repeatedly avoided capture. During the chase, this uncle managed to slip and fall into the incredibly foul pig manure, and rolled around in it like a corncob in butter. We all laughed, even my cousin's mother and father, and his sisters roared. The pig, however, was ultimately caught and cooked.

It was painful to be in their presence for too long. This uncle was beyond taciturn for he only spoke by dropping "gems" at irregular intervals. When one of these was arriving, his wife would hush us by saying uncle was about to speak. Since we had lots to say, this hushing could take some time. With a build up like this, we should have expected the Gettysburg Address, but all we got were banalities coated with meanness delivered in an authoritarian tone.

There was something more, something I'm almost too embarrassed to write. When we were in their house, and we rarely went in alone, this aunt would threaten us in what she might have thought was a playful manner. Under the kitchen floor was a dark, dank earthen hole accessible only through a trapdoor—we never went there. Looking directly at us, she promised to put us down there with the "nigger" if we didn't behave. With some adornments, she repeated this bizarre story about the "nigger" for years; this story is the main reason we enjoyed wrapping the garter snake around her neck in that futile attempt to cure a goiter. Now none of us had seen a black person, so we had no reason to be prejudiced. On the rare occasions when this uncle dropped a gem, he would add to her strange story. Somewhere they had picked up this prejudice meme that dovetailed with their view of life.

This uncle's house was an unhappy place; they all died young, his wife at just 47. After they were gone, their son, the cousin who discovered the woodcock's nest, burnt the house to the ground one night while, drunk, he sat on a stone pile laughing uproariously. He said it was the best night of his life!

All this "nigger" stuff was nonsense, of course! No one I knew thought like that. Years after my dad left, chasing a bottle of whiskey, Mother lived in Malawi (Nyasaland), Africa, with her boyfriend. He was building sawmills for CIDA (Canadian International Development Agency) and training the locals to operate them. Mother recalls having a grand time working side by side with the Africans; it reminded her of her years as a cook in the lumber camps when I was a child.

Oh, I would like to think my cousin and I were like Huckleberry Finn raised wild and without the prejudices of "civilized" society. We weren't angels, but we weren't devils either. Mark Twain paints an immortal scene of Huck and Jim, the runaway slave, on the Mississippi River. Huck had left Jim on the raft under a pretext and headed off in their canoe. He had a storm in his head between what society, the school, and the church taught and what his natural morality told him: should he betray their friendship and give Jim up to authorities or not? Let's listen in to how Mark Twain tells it in Chapter 16 of *The Adventures of Huckleberry Finn*:

> Well, I just felt sick. But I says, I *got* to do it—I can't get *out* of it. Right then along comes a skiff with two men in it with guns, and they stopped and I stopped. One of them says:
> "What's that yonder?"
> "A piece of a raft," I says.
> "Do you belong on it?"
> "Yes, sir."
> "Any men on it?"
> "Only one, sir."
> "Well, there's five niggers run off to-night up yonder, above the head of the bend. Is your man white or black?"
> I didn't answer up prompt. I tried to, but the words wouldn't come. I tried for a second or two to brace up and out with it, but I warn't man enough—hadn't the spunk of a rabbit. I see I was weakening; so I just give up trying, and up and says:
> "He's white."

Sparrow Hawk

As I mentioned earlier, we had no books, magazines, or newspapers, but we had our small colored calendar with a picture of a sparrow hawk's head for May (*see* photo). We saw these gorgeous birds from time to time on telephone wires when my uncle drove us to town. Even with the keen eyesight of youth, we still needed binoculars for a detailed look.

Kestrel Falcon

It turns out this bird is not a hawk but a falcon and its correct name is kestrel. These small birds and their larger cousins, the merlin and the peregrine, catch prey with speed—the last is the world's fastest flyer.

When I built my home on the back 40 acres, I also built a few nest boxes for kestrels, and one was used. Often the parents collected so much food—mice, voles, grasshoppers, and so on—that their babies could eat no more. In that case, the parents laid the surplus on top of my swallow and bluebird houses for a later meal.

As boys, my cousin and I had no book knowledge of hawks, and no way of acquiring any. Once while we were walking through the forest near Walden Pond—it was a cranberry bog then—two large chunky birds jumped from the lower branches of a tree and scurried off through the undergrowth. Although we doubled our chances by each pursuing a separate bird, they eluded us. At that time, we didn't know what they were, but I now feel certain they were red-tailed hawklets. It's normal for them to leave the nest before they can fly and roost on nearby branches; the parents, of course, still feed them.

Other than the red-tail hawk and the kestrel falcon, we saw no raptors. I count us boys as keen observers of all wildlife, so the question I must ask myself now is where all the other raptors—hawks, falcons, and eagles—were. Clearly, it was not because we weren't looking that we missed them, that's what we did all day. One part of the answer is DDT. At the lumber mill, the men would spray their sleeping quarters with vast quantities of DDT. Amid a potent mixture of sweat from their labors, smoke from their pipes and cigarettes, plus this insecticide, the men slept. It's a wonder any of them, forget the mosquitos, lived through the night. In 1962, Rachel Carson brought the dangers of pesticides to national attention and started the environmental movement with her apocalyptic book *Silent Spring*.

Then there was a second problem—owls, hawks, falcons, and eagles had a bad reputation. They killed other birds, not just chickens but those sweet little birds we all liked. And not everyone was a poor shot like my uncle with the .22. Tens of thousands of raptors were slaughtered annually, especially at migration sites where they tend to concentrate. Even major figures involved with conservation joined in the killing. We know humans can behave badly toward other humans, look at the world wars, so cruelty toward other beasts and birds is no surprise. Some humans, hopefully most, have come to their senses and our better angels have taken charge. With the banning of DDT in the 70s and the protection of all birds of prey presently, hawks, falcons, and eagles have returned to give balance, beauty, and majesty to nature. A forest without wildlife is just landscape.

The true hawks, the accipiters, came back first. They employ stealth, speed, and maneuverability in the forest to catch prey. They come in three sizes: small, medium, and large or sharp-shinned, cooper's, and goshawk respectively. Presently, the farm has all three, and my cousin and I were there to greet them.

Mature Cooper's Hawk

Immature Cooper's Hawk

We are older now and as close to being mature as we can get or want. Three bush cords of cut and split maple, beech, and ash dumped in a jumbled pile lay beside my newly built cabin. My cousin had come to help me pile the wood, as he said "correctly." He meant crisscrossing the end pieces to construct stand-alone supports for the wood piled between.

The first mists of morning filled the east, and the fog rose out of the valley below, yet we could hear the fall migration of Canada geese as they talked to each other in the distance. Before long, a young cooper's hawk appeared and hid in some old maples on the edge of the field. Because we adults had binoculars, we took a good long look. The vertical chest marks and yellow eyes of an adolescent cooper's hawk contrast boldly with the adult's horizontal stripes and blood-red eyes (*see* respective photos). Born last spring, the immature hawk we saw was migrating south for the first time.

A flock of ten or so blue jays was nearby. We stopped piling wood and watched. What would each bird do? Before long, the hawk dove at the jays on the ground scattering them, and that should have been the end of it. But teasingly the jays perched nearby in the surrounding trees and the hawk repeatedly dive-bombed each. Miss! Miss! Miss! This continued for some time, until my cousin and I had to conclude the blue jays were mocking the hawk and just having fun. Dangerous for them, but not so dangerous as to make them leave the field of combat. Doubtless, the hawk thought otherwise; he was just hungry.

Perhaps the jays knew this cooper's hawk was inexperienced. I never saw this behavior in the spring when all the birds were mature—but it happened every fall thereafter. My cousin reminisced about the time we hid on the hillside and watched a den of fox kits play. Humans are not the only animals that enjoy playing. Playfulness is a tribute to animals' *joie de vivre* or joy of living; they're like Zorba the Greek, dancing with disaster.

Refreshed after this entertainment, we returned to piling the firewood. When we were almost finished my cousin, who was always quick with the quip, handed me the last stick of wood and said, "Here's the piece you've been looking for." It had been a grand autumn day of "mists and mellow fruitfulness," as John Keats wrote. That New Year's Eve my cousin died!

Adult American Bald Eagle

It was another decade before the eagles returned. In places, rock fences interspersed with ancient sugar maple trees separate the two farms. It was late fall and the migration was over; the bears had gone into hibernation—the land seemed emptied of all life.

I had taken up the yearly practice of feeding wolves with road-killed deer attempting to photograph them in my camera traps. Initially the ravens arrive to feast, a hundred or so, and on this unique day my first eagle. He sat majestically in the ancient maples and watched Babylon below as the ravens squabbled and jostled over the carcass.

The eagle was at a distance of 300 yards (275 m) from my home, so I photographed his magnificence from comfort. Unsatisfied with the resolution, I grabbed my Nikon camera, opened the door, and walked toward him to see how close he would allow me to approach. Instantly, the ravens departed, but the eagle held his ground. Closer—photo! Closer still—another photo! Finally, I was at the base of the maple looking up in reverence at the majesty and power that is the adult bald eagle (*see* photo). He stared straight at me fearless and unblinking: wild nature met human nature and only one of us was impressed.

The ravens immediately returned when I left, but the eagle did not eat that day. Eagles sometimes wait for hours or even days before descending and grasping a huge piece of meat or fat and flying off with a retinue of ravens in pursuit. On other days,

Eagle and Ravens

the eagle joined the jostling masses on the ground; the ravens give the eagle a wide birth lest they become desert. Nonetheless, some brave or foolish raven doubtless to impress the others, will always pull the eagle's tail.

Eagle at Lunch

It was another half-dozen years before a golden eagle came to the farm and landed in the same maple tree. These birds are rare in the east, migrating out of the province most winters. As the

Immature Bald Eagle   Golden Eagle

bald eagle doesn't achieve the entirely white head until its fifth year, it can be mistaken for a golden (*see* photographs comparing these). Although bald eagles, both juvenile and adult, became winter regulars and summer occasional sky circlers, the golden eagle was an erratic fall migrant.

I had two regular spots where the deer carcasses were placed. One was near my cousin's headstone, and the other deep in the woods. Now it was mere foolishness for me to put the bait near his burial site, but I did it anyway. Somehow, it felt better when I did this because the eagles he never saw in life were now close to him in death. As I said, it was mere foolishness!

The golden eagle came in November, and never again that year. My bird books—I now have as least 20—tell me these birds breed in Ungava, Quebec, near the high Arctic. One of these "babies" sat to have its photograph taken by my camera trap (*see* "First-Year Golden Eagle"). The white at the base of the tail indicates it was born the previous spring. In their second year, this color is replaced by brown. All female raptors are larger than their male counterparts. This bird may be a female. Clearly, it's large and the talons are impressive. Goldens normally don't eat carrion, but, as I said, the land seemed emptied of life, and this meat was merely frozen.

First-Year Golden Eagle

Evolution by natural selection has equipped all these raptors with unique anatomical features. Owls fly on wings whose tips are so delicately feathered that prey cannot hear their approach. Vultures have the best sense of smell in the avian world. Hawks have incredible eyesight and maneuverability in tight quarters. And eagles[*] have amazing vision, strength, and gripping power. Natural selection—descent with modification as Darwin said—created all these features, and a thousand more, without a plan, without a purpose, and without foresight, to cope with the here and now.

Scientists have every reason to expect natural selection to work throughout the entire Laniakea, indeed throughout the cosmos. If on some other "earth" in a galaxy far, far away there is life, it will be hard pressed to produce anything more grand than the creatures on our earth. And in reverence for this life, we need to protect all species against those who would destroy them because of ignorance and callousness for profit and "sport."

As David Attenborough writes, "It seems to me that the natural world is the greatest source of excitement; the greatest source of visual beauty; the greatest source of intellectual interest. It is the greatest source of so much in life that makes life worth living." [•]

And then to awake, and the farm, like a wanderer white
With the dew, come back, the cock on his shoulder: it was all
Shining, it was Adam and maiden,
The sky gathered again
And the sun grew round that very day.
Dylan Thomas, "Fern Hill"

---

[*] Search "Gordon Harrison Adult Bald Eagle" for my YouTube video.
[•] David Attenborough, quoted in *Wildlife Film-Making: Looking to the Future*, by Piers Warren (London, UK: Wildeye, 2011), 30.

CHAPTER—17

NORTH WOODS RUNNERS

*Grandmother lived out in the wood, half a league from the village,
and just as Little Red-Cap entered the wood, a wolf met her.
Red-Cap did not know what a wicked creature he was,
and was not at all afraid of him.*
Brothers Grimm, "Little Red-Cap [Little Red Riding Hood]"

An amber glow shone from the window of the house with the two staircases on a cool summer evening; four children huddled around a man listening to his stories. Their only lamp cast no heat, but that didn't matter for they were listening intently as he recounted another of his hunting adventures. It could have been a scene out of central Asia with everyone gathered around a campfire telling tales of the day's bear hunt, for the broad outline of these tales is always the same. The hero goes forth on a dangerous quest; he meets his adversary, engages him in battle, and defeats him, returning home in triumph.

The Algonquin Wolf

In much of the world, the evil adversary has been the wolf—top predators always dislike each other. My uncle was a superb teller of tall tales; his enthusiasm and conviction were contagious. Whether the stories were true really didn't matter to us children. Yet, in all of his encounters with wolves—and he spent most of his life outdoors—he never spoke of killing one. If I close my eyes, I can be there again lost in rapture with my imagination adding the color and sound to his Homeric tales.

At the dramatic climax, my cousin's sisters would often become frightened and run to their mother, who was putting away the supper dishes. Although my cousin and his sisters were all the same age—*they were triplets*—the girls rarely went outdoors by themselves and never into the forest. They had a different life.

After an hour or so of these narratives, we would become aware of the slight hiss of the Aladdin mantle lamp. My uncle always returned the hero by virtue of his surviving the wolves tracking him or surrounding him at his campfire. He had no hatred toward wolves just respect for a worthy adversary, so my cousin and I had none as well. But of all creatures on the farm, the wolves gripped our imagination in a way words cannot express. After the stories, many of which we had heard before, my cousin and I would go up the stairs, stroke the owl's head, and lie down to dream of our quests and encounters with wolves.

Outside the house, all the farm animals were sleeping. The barns bathed in the gray stillness of moonlight or the faint glow of the stars appeared otherworldly. The horses in their stanchions slept standing up with locked knees. In another barn, the geese and ducks wiggled a nest in some straw while the chickens and turkeys took to the highest roosts they could find. The pigeons were asleep in the loft of the post-and-beam barn. And the pigs, after having rolled in more mud against late-summer mosquitoes, were "cuddled" in a small group in their large outdoor enclosure. But the cows were elsewhere on the farm no doubt at the crest of some rise lying in a rough circle, sleeping but aware of predators. Wolves particularly spooked them.

Nonetheless, not every creature was sleeping: the barn cats were stalking mice while the mice were searching for food. Some large milk snakes in the haymow were also hunting mice. Life was everywhere but it was quiet, secretive.

Beyond the barns, in the spring field, the slash, the little fallow field, and further still was a noisy quietness. Nighthawks flying over the fields would occasionally see a ghostly figure move from grove to forest—possibly a bear, deer, moose, fox, fisher, or even a wolf. At the furthest end of the farm in a valley we called the back-barn flat, we had another large two-story structure in which hay was stored. On this August night just after midnight, a pack of wolves furious with life rushed out of the tall hemlock forest to the south to cross this open area. There were seven; this year's pups were on a training run.

Young Algonquin Wolf

Sleeping, we of course knew nothing of this. Yet in the decades to come when I had built my home at the top of the hill, above the back-barn flat, I came to realize this area was a well-used runway. On hundreds of nights, wolves would wake me with their astonishing howls[*]—and this great wilderness song moved me profoundly. Here was a creature that didn't need us and lived free in a way humans hadn't for ten millennia. They have their own families, their own moral values, and as we will see their own wild justice.

Even as boys, my cousin and I had an encounter with this wolf runway across the back-barn flat and into the forest. It happened on a berry-picking expedition that included all the women and girls in the family: my mother, our grandmother, my aunt, and my cousin's two sisters. We went along. Although we weren't good pickers, we were excellent eaters. My mother and aunt had large cans while grandmother had a pail; the rest of us had little tins the size of two cups. Apparently, our picking reputations preceded us. Our grandmother was a legendary picker—she would pick after us and get a quart while we got a handful,

[*] Listen to the Eastern Wolf on the website *The Science Behind Algonquin's Animals* and be amazed (www.sbaa.ca/projects.asp?cn=314).

or should I say mouthful. Today we were collecting wild strawberries, not the genetically modified kind found in today's supermarket but tiny things the size of a few apple seeds suitable
for chipmunks. We soon tired of this and decided to leave for
other adventures. As it turned out, we were picking where my
home now stands. In those days, the fields were so open you
could see the entire flat and the barn below.

We said our goodbyes, and I'm certain our grandmother
thought we were no loss to this project. Down the hill we went to
explore a large spring bubbling out of the hillside and forming a
rivulet that ended in a pool. And the pool was home to frogs, tadpoles, and other aquatic life. The adults saw us leave, but my
cousin's sisters clung closely to the skirts of the berry pickers. Arriving at this permanent pool, my cousin and I found it alive with
large green frog tadpoles that, like bullfrog larva, spend two years
growing up. Each tadpole was the size and shape of a plum; we
considered them wonders to watch and treasures to own. We still
had our empty berry cans, but the tadpoles proved to be too quick
for us to catch.

Just then, the berry pickers cried, "Wolf!" "Wolf!" "Wolf!"
We were on the ancient wolf pathway that I came to know decades later. Their warning was clear and because of the water
from the spring, the foliage was thick so we hid behind a large
gathering of ferns. No sooner were we hidden, than three adult

Fall Wolf by my Home

wolves appeared, had a cool drink, and continued up the heavily forested valley toward Walker's Brook. If my cousin and I should live a 1000 years, we would never again have such a great view of these magnificent animals. Perhaps we were downwind of them so they missed our scent, yet they must have heard the adults cry wolf*. Breathless my mother and aunt arrived minutes later frantic with fear and concern to find two smiling and proud boys with a story equal to any of my uncle's. No one was as impressed as we were, all else was fear!

In all human societies, we are the super predator and we will tolerate no competition. In reshaping the earth closer to the heart's desire, we have exterminated for eternity thousands of species. Wolves generally live in a balance with nature. If they kill all their prey, they die as well by starvation. Not so for humans; we just change the menu items. Hopefully, there will come a time when we will be ashamed of our extermination of life on earth.

Which Bone to Pick?

We are at the top of the food chain, and other animals best not forget our ascendancy. Wolves learned this lesson early on when humans first invented the gun; since then, these canids have strictly avoided humans. Most people in my area have never seen a wolf, nor are they likely to. It little profits a wolf to meet a man. The former is always a loser to the latter.

Dogs are just friendly wolves . . . mostly. In Asia, some 25,000 years ago or more, some wolves began following our hunter-gatherer

* All the photographs in this chapter were shot on the farm of completely wild wolves—no compounds, zoos, or enclosures. *Search* "Gordon Harrison Two Algonquin Wolves" for one of my YouTube videos.

264 / My Cousin & Me

ancestors, and a few went over to the human side. The hunters had been fortunate and killed several deer, so scraps of meat and bones were plentiful around the camp. These few brave wolves crept close to take advantage of this unique ecological niche. The hunters recognized their value as an early warning system against bears, lions, hyenas, and other predators. Soon the hunters purposefully fed them leftovers. One cold night a wolf less afraid than the others came close to the fire for warmth. And a brave young man more bold than others reached out his hand and stroked the wolf's back, and, with that, the family dog was born! Still not all subspecies of wolf can be tamed; the African wild dog is one such. Even if you get one as a pup, they are unmanageable, just as zebras cannot be domesticated.

As we have seen, the genetic pool of the common pigeon is incredibly rich. It was fertile enough to breed hundreds of new subspecies by artificial selection. Yet the speciation of wolves may be even larger. Presently there are more than 300 breeds of dog, ranging in height from the Chihuahua to the Irish wolfhound all derived from a few friendly wolves.

Interestingly, even with an immense gene pool, all the wolves in my area tend to look alike, as do the wild pigeons. These are not the large gray wolves of the boreal forest and beyond, nor are they the smaller coyotes of the south. They're a separate race variously called the eastern Canadian wolf, the Algonquin wolf, or, more exactly, *Canis lycaon*—a subspecies of the US red wolf.

Eastern Canadian Wolf: *Canis lycaon*

Appearance alone implies some hybridization among the Algonquin wolf, the gray wolf, and coyotes. This upsets purists; I wonder why? Mark Twain has the following to say about his dog Jasper:

> He wa'n't no common dog, he wa'n't no mongrel; he was a composite. A composite dog is a dog that's made up of all the valuable qualities that's in the dog breed—kind of a syndicate; and a mongrel is made up of all riffraff that's left over.

And, yes, composites are often hardier and stronger. All the dogs my cousin and I had on the farm were composites with the strength and endurance of mules. We were limited in our naming: there were two "Pals," one "Cubby," and three "Queenies," but only one was my hound at the mill on the lake. In truth, all life-forms are composites. And the search for racial purity is a search for unicorns—and they're composites too.

Composites have their boundaries, however. Biologists define species as the largest group of organisms capable of interbreeding and producing fertile offspring. All legends and myths of interspecies mating and producing fertile offspring with body parts of each "parent" are mere foolishness. For example, consider the wolf-deer or wolder (*see* photo) with the head of a deer on the body of a wolf. These "exist" only in Photoshop.

The Mythical Wolder

On the Origin of Species describes the eastern Canadian wolf as being a lightly built, greyhound-like animal that pursued deer, as opposed to the bulkier, shorter-legged gray wolf. The fur has some cinnamon coloring, especially behind the ears. Black-colored wolves are extremely rare. I have seen and photographed only one (pictured here).

A Black Algonquin Wolf at Walden Pond

To know the exact relationship among gray wolves, Algonquin wolves, and coyotes, you would need a detailed genetic analysis, and I have none of that. In its place, I offer a simple diptych (*see* photos) in which I see a progression from coyote-like to wolf-like, indicating that the Algonquin wolf (aka the eastern Canadian wolf) is a composite of both.

More Coyote-Like   More Wolf-Like

As noted previously, morality arises in a social context, and even hermits have a need for it in their relationship with nature's wild creatures. All herd or pack animals have a large moral repertoire: whales, dolphins, elephants, and wolves.

For example, if the time and place should require it, wolves will stand with their pack mates to face another pack, a bear, or any enemy. This is not an idle statement because all their prosocial behavior has prepared them for this gladiatorial moment—they will stand and deliver—even the young!

Young Algonquin Wolf

When I first moved into my new home on the back 40, there was a den of wolves not far west of me (*see* map page 288). Every evening when my dog Ruffy and I would go for our last walk of the day, he would stop periodically and look off into the impenetrable forest. Almost immediately the wolves would howl as if

Pack of Four Wolves by My Home

to say we know you are there—come no closer. (Wolves can smell 100 times more acutely than humans.) Clearly, Ruffy also knew the wolves were there. I, of course, knew nothing. Occasionally during the daytime, I would see a wolf carrying a rabbit or woodchuck back to its den to feed the pups. Excluding these pups, I believe there were just four adults in the pack. My first camera trap used film and it captured the night photograph (reproduced here) of four wolves—count the eyes.

Deer are not the only food item on the wolf's menu. As noted, they regularly take small game, even mice and squirrels, but their second food choice is beaver. These rodents can grow to unexpected sizes with 44 pounds (20 kg) being typical, and they constitute 40 percent of the wolf's diet. If Grey Owl and Anahareo (Chapter 10) hadn't saved the beaver from extinction, we would have lost most of our wolves, another reason beavers are a keystone species.

Those Damn Ravens

The third item on the wolf's menu wasn't on the farm in my childhood and youth. Or, if it were, my cousin and I never saw one, although there was a story of some relative or other

—we had a large family—shooting one. In recent decades these animals have taken over much of Algonquin Park, displacing the white-tailed deer, and are now quite common on the farm. I consider them our most dangerous animal especially the female with child. They know no fear, but they can deliver it! Some people are unaware that they are the largest member of the *deer family*. We call them moose.

The male (bull) is generally too large for wolves to take down unless it is weakened by disease or prolonged pursuit. The moose's best defense is to stand its ground—one kick from the cloven hoof of a moose can kill a wolf or a man.

Bull Moose

When I met the magnificent bull moose pictured here, I was alone. My dog Ruffy was on the Happy Isles where all brave and loyal dogs go. His absence was fortunate because moose mistake dogs for wolves and become aggressive. This bull appeared relaxed and posed as I took his photograph again and again. Yousuf Karsh couldn't have asked for a better subject. After several minutes of posing, he tired and turned to amble away, and, as he did, I followed. This was a mistake because he interpreted my act as hostile and quickly let me know. Sometime later after he left, I climbed down the tree and quickly walked home without seeing him again.

Wolves generally kill the old, the weak, and the young, and by so doing they keep their prey in top form. A moose calf is a favorite; the only problem for the wolves is mother (the cow) and her lethal hooves.

Moose Calf and Cow at the Left

Prey are never helpless. That's not how evolution proceeds. If the wolves get stronger and faster, so do the deer in a kind of arms race. Also, deer can fight as well as run! Antlers and hooves are deadly! Most wolf chases are unsuccessful. Wolves hunt the way our ancestors did on the African savannah, achieving success by persistence—that is they run their prey to exhaustion. With long legs, a lean body, and large paws (*see* photo of wolf prints), wolves are built to run in the snow for up to 25 miles (40 km) regularly. If the wolves can keep the deer within sight, the hunt is generally

Wolf Prints in the Snow

successful. Every winter I find kill sites on lakes and ponds, and often on the ancient runway at the bottom of my hill where my cousin and I saw three wolves as we hid spellbound in some ferns.

Nonetheless, especially in the fall before the snow arrives, wolves are starving, some close to death. At this juncture, these carnivores will eat anything including windfall fruit from the trees in my orchard. The emaciated wolf pictured here was devouring fallen plums, as many as he could find, and glancing up at the tree for more. (*See* "Young Wolf in My Orchard" for a photograph showing how thin he was.)

Young Wolf in My Orchard

The eyes of all animals—this includes you and me—are highly evolved. Charles Darwin himself acknowledges in *On the Origin of Species* that it seems absurd to think the eye formed by natural selection. Yet he firmly believed it did evolve in that way, despite a lack of evidence at the time[*]. Life provides a stunning array of

---

[*] For a complete explanation, see *Climbing Mount Improbable* by Richard Dawkins.

different eyes, implying the eye evolved many times, from the compound eyes of insects to the phenomenal vision of octopuses.

Without realizing it, my cousin and I noticed a unique ability in the eyes of nocturnal animals. While traveling to the farm on a dark summer night, we would scan the road ahead for the reflected glare of the car's headlights in animals' eyes. The classic case is the "caught in the headlights" look of deer or a family of raccoons. Unlike my father, my uncle never hit an animal or tried to. On other occasions, we would see light reflected by the eyes of rabbits and skunks and, very rarely, a beaver or even a wolf (*see* "Wolf with White-Eye"). With each sighting, we became excited naming hills and valleys in each animal's honor. These names will never be found on any map or anywhere else but in my memory. So *Skunk Hill* and *Raccoon Hollow* still live every time I drive over them. We were children who would not color within the lines or follow tradition. Dylan Thomas expresses this sentiment best in *A Child's Christmas in Wales*:

> [A]nd a painting book in which I could make the grass, the trees, the sea and the animals any color I please, and still the dazzling sky-blue sheep are grazing in the red field under the rainbow-billed and pea-green birds.

Wolf with White-Eye

In the natural world, nocturnal animals have evolved a "straight-back" concave reflector. This reflector—a layer of cells behind the retina called the *tapetum lucidum*—gives the animal "white-eye." As this cellular layer is absent in humans, we get "red-eye" from a network of blood vessels. The purpose of the *tapetum* is to reflect light back through the rods of the retina a second time, thereby giving creatures like wolves and foxes excellent night vision. Each photon is reflected straight back to the same photocell that missed it coming the other way so the image is not distorted. If the photon is missed on this second try, it escapes the eye socket and becomes part of the white-eye phenomenon.

As boys, my cousin and I knew none of this. Yet knowing now does not diminish or subtract from the excitement I still feel every time the light from my truck's headlights or my flashlight is reflected straight back to me from eyes that say, "I see you too."

Wolf and Ravens at Deer-Kill Site

Wolves have a unique and ancient relationship with another animal—find one and you will soon find the other. They help each other in ways I suspect neither would admit to. So close is this symbiotic relationship between wolves and ravens* that the latter is regularly called the wolf-bird. And they talk to each other, or at least the ravens call and the wolves listen.

Let me explain a little of what I've learned about raven society from observation and from reading Bernd Heinrich's marvelous book *Ravens in Winter*. Raven society has two levels: resident pairs and roving bands of juveniles. The resident pair claims a large territory as its own where the two raise their family and gather their food. And they can rule this territory for 20 or more years, vigorously driving out all intruders in spectacular aerial chases and fights.

Scouting expeditions cover hundreds of miles, but all the birds normally return to a roost tree for the night. Over the last two decades, a few of these temporary roost trees have been near my home, and the ravens that gather there, rather than rest let alone sleep, have what sounds like an all-night rock party. A honeybee that has found a large cluster of new flowers will lead its hive mates to them; surprisingly ravens do something similar. In an apparent act of altruism, the bird who finds a carcass will lead his flock mates to the site from the roost tree.

The Raven

* Watch "Gordon Harrison What Does the Wolf Say?"—my YouTube video on wolf-raven interactions at a deer-kill site.

As you might expect, this unusual altruism among *unrelated* birds aroused great interest in researcher Bernd Heinrich.

His explanation was cogent, but not easily discovered. It turns out that, if a roving juvenile finds a carcass, you can be certain the resident pair for that area has also found it. This pair would instantly drive off a single juvenile raven, but if a gang of ten or more arrives, the pair gives up and takes what it can from the carcass. If the wolves haven't opened the carcass, no one gets much; even ravens' oversized bills can't penetrate deer or moose hide (*see* pictured profile of the raven). What to do? Well, ravens have an ancient solution! These birds produce a particularly loud ruckus call that summons any wolf within miles. Then everyone eats. As I said, ravens call and wolves listen.

Ravens may well be the world's most intelligent bird; they live from the high Arctic to Death Valley and everywhere in between. Because they have a vocabulary of 65 or more words, we are just beginning to learn their language. Several times larger than crows and much, much smarter, they have phenomenal problem solving abilities.

Running Wolf

And they play, they play a lot. They will pull the eagle's feathers and the wolf's tail. I suspect the ravens that do these things are males attempting to impress females in the juvenile gang. These gangs are a kind of dating service until two mate and fly off to claim their own territory. I have seen them make repeated snow angels creating the impression of a giant dinosaur's rib cage. Like children, they tuck in their wings and slide down hills squawking happily all the way. In the sky, they dive, tumble, twirl, and do such things you dare not dream of. They are tricksters, daredevils, and acrobats. And, along with wolves, they are two of Darwin's greatest descendants.

So let the wolves run on through the evergreen forests in their eternal pursuit of the deer. The mindless mote of carbon we met in chapter one that traveled the entire Laniakea was absorbed in the growth of a flower that was eaten by a yearling deer who in turn was devoured by wolves. Now the mote is running with the wolves somewhere in this vast land, perhaps as part of the front leg of the alpha male in a powerful pack (*see* "Running Wolf").

A forest without wildlife is just a landscape!
A wood without wolves is just a city park!
And a life without animals is just a tea party!

CHAPTER—18

THE LAND BETWEEN

I should hear him fly with the high fields
And wake to the farm forever fled from the childless land.
Oh as I was young and easy in the mercy of his means,
Time held me green and dying
Though I sang in my chains like the sea.
Dylan Thomas, "Fern Hill"

Humans have none of the special abilities of the animals we have met. We cannot run as fast as deer nor see as clearly as eagles, nor have we any of a thousand other gifts of natural selection. So why do we dominate the environment? The late Jacob Bronowski answers this question in the first paragraph of his magnificent book *The Ascent of Man*:

> Man is a singular creature. He has a set of gifts which make him unique among the animals, so that, unlike them, he is not a figure in the landscape—he is the shaper of the landscape. In body and in mind he is the explorer of nature, the ubiquitous animal, who did not find but made his home in every continent.

We may build our homes on every continent, as Bronowski says, and in every environment too, but many of these environments are severe, even hostile places to live. And we can survive in Antarctica or outer space and everywhere in between only because we change that environment. The universe is large and full of wonders, but I need to know this place, the farm, for the first time: know its animals and people, its beauty and hardships. In this final chapter, we will look at the humans who came to this stern land and cut down the forests to fashion a life for themselves.

In the last two centuries, a new creature has lived on the land near the Red Spot, an animal who by labor and passion thought to mold this rocky wilderness closer to the heart's desire. Like Sisyphus, these creatures would roll the rocks into piles and fences, cut the trees into houses and barns, and scratch the fields with shovels and plows to grow a few vegetables. Since time is the overlord of all ventures, these hardy, brave, and foolish pioneers are all gone now, as are their houses and fields. They were our people—my cousin's and mine.

> *And where the farms are*
> *it's as if a man stuck*
> *both thumbs in the stony earth and pulled*
> *it apart*
> *to make room*
> *enough between the trees*
> *for a wife*
> *and maybe some cows and*
> *room for some*
> *of the more easily kept illusions—*
> Al Purdy, "The Country North of Belleville"

None of us, including Native Americans, are truly indigenous to the New World. We all came here from elsewhere. My great grandparents arrived in Canada from Northern Ireland and Scotland; my cousin and I listened to many a Scottish song or verse lovingly recited by our grandmother. She was Scottish and proud of it. Although the photograph of me with my grandparents is many decades old, I believe I can detect a slight smile on her

My Grandfather, Grandmother, and the Author

face—grandfather, sadly, died the following winter so I was too young to know him.

At the right side of the picture is one of the farm's many barns. My mother, always the one to try something new, had a Brownie, the name of a popular and simple camera. If she had not owned this camera, I would have no photos of the farm to conjure up a million memories.

This "Land Between" is where two iconic environments collided, the Canadian Shield and the St. Lawrence Lowlands, to create a vast area rich in plants, animals, and people—the best of both ecosystems. My great-grandparents emigrated from the Old World to this place. They must have been traveling light because they carried no keepsakes of any kind, no mementos of their previous life, nor, I was told, did they ever speak of it. The men were soldiers returned from the horrors of war, and some things were best forgotten. They went forth naked to live life on their own terms in a new land. As the minstrel sang:

> *Long live the pioneers*
> . . . .
> *Go forth and have no fear*

The land was free if you maintained the logging roads on either side; otherwise, it was 50 cents an acre. My people took the first option. At the end of one of these roads was the mill where my mother was the cook and my father a blacksmith. The government threw these colonists onto the land with some imaginary plans to farm these rocks buttered with soil. Some survived, some perished, most left. Fortunately, my people endured and I would even say thrived.

The original log cabin my great-grandfather built to endure that first terrible winter has completely gone back to nature. My cousin and I searched diligently for any remains following the rough directions of our grandmother—whom I'm certain never saw it either. Its putative location was near the mysterious lake and marsh where we saw the mink, and not far from Mother Courage's final den. I can well imagine that my great-grandfather's labor was intense, but hard work was something he already knew. We can also safely assume the experience of owning land was exhilarating. In the early morning, looking out over this ancient glacial lake to see deer, bear, and wolf come down to drink, he knew he was the lord of all the beauty he surveyed:

> *Bush land scrub land—*
> . . . .
> *where a man might have some*
> *opinion of what beauty*
> *is and none deny him*
> *for miles*

Al Purdy, "The Country North of Belleville"

The Survivors
Picture courtesy of *The Land Between*

By hand axe, my great-grandfather cleared a road past the mysterious lake (*see* map on page 288) to the back half of his farm. It's along this road that my cousin and I scared up a thousand partridge and sat mesmerized by gilled salamanders swimming in shallow pools of sunshine. With hand saw and horse, he also built a permanent home on the land he cleared at the crest of a rise set against the sky as you come up the road. (My home now stands on this same rise.) In the year 1900, the barn now being swallowed by the forest was erected. He married a local girl and had a large family, one of whom was my grandfather.

Logs Gathered for Some Ghost Purpose

The farmers bartered goods, but to earn cash they had to work in the lumber camps and mill. Our grandfather went to work in these camps at nine years of age. These epic family stories were the traditions on which my cousin and I nursed.

We might have asked where our great-grandfather came from. Yes, I know the proximal answer was Ireland and Scotland for my great-grandmother, but they were ultimately immigrants there also. Where did our ancestors truly come from? Where? The future will not be like the past. Tomorrow will not be like today. Every day is different. And most are better. My life was not like the life of my parents, and theirs was different from their parents. If we could follow this trail of ancestors far enough back in time, where would it lead? *Fortunately, we can know!*

The National Geographic Society is collecting DNA samples (mouth swabs) from every continent to create the earth's first "genographic" map showing the migration routes of all peoples out of Africa approximately 65,000 years ago. That's about 2,000 generations, not long enough for any major genetic variation to occur. If readers wish to know their deep ancestry, search "genographic" and participate in this landmark study. Add your DNA to this unique map of the continental wanderings of humankind.

My Maternal Line: Out of Africa

As you can see by the map, I have had my DNA analyzed to learn my deep maternal ancestry. Some 65,000 years ago, my people left an area near Lake Victoria, Africa, on an epic journey that ended on the farm! (*See* the red pointer.) Follow these red spots to see my family's journey. Offshoot arrows are for other families. Although it is not on the map, *the final Red spot is on my front lawn!* This journey, this larger-than-life trek, began during the last ice age when sea levels were much lower. Following game, my ancestors were able to cross from Africa into Asia somewhere over what is now the Red Sea. Rather than turn west they went east to the Caspian Sea before turning north and then west into present-day Germany. From here they split again, trekking to Italy, France, and England and, ultimately, to Scotland and Ireland and, of course, to The Land Between. This epic 65,000-year journey required extraordinary intelligence and greatness of the human spirit. They were fearless! I am humbled! Absolutely humbled!

None of this journey is conjecture; it's supported by the special mutations called markers by geneticists. Your DNA contains the greatest history book ever written—a kind of time machine. We are all one tremendous family; ideas of race are false, totally false! We are all Africans.

Who were those who stayed behind in Africa? Fortunately, we know that too. They were the San people of the remote and hostile Kalahari Desert. Dr. Spencer Wells, who runs the genographic project, claims he can see Asians, Australians, Indians, and Europeans in the faces of the San. Like the pigeons and the wolves, their genome is incredibly rich. The San are ancestors to all of us. On the tree of life, if we are the tips of the branches, they are the trunk.

San People of the Kalahari—Ancient Rock Painting

When the rock painting pictured here came into my possession, I took it to the Royal Ontario Museum to verify its authenticity. Their experts affirmed it was a San rock painting and very ancient. They pointed to the flaking on some figures, which is unusual considering the very long-lasting paints they used.

Science has discovered many deep truths in recent decades. And, surprisingly, a few of these truths have profound moral implications. *We are a part of, not apart from, nature.* We, like all of Darwin's descendants, are another creature in the landscape even if we shape that landscape. If you think otherwise, you have been left behind and are out of touch with the best idea anyone ever had: natural selection.

All recorded human events, what we call history, account for such a minuscule span of time that the period could almost be overlooked. But prehistory, and particularly pre-prehistory, is where the action happened. Here the panoply of life on earth unfolded. Here life originated and started on its immense evolutionary journey.

The latest research indicates that life began at least 3.6 billion years ago in the Precambrian era. Now ages or numbers of that magnitude are just black marks on white paper. Human beings, still living on average the biblical lifespan of three score and ten years, have no psychological or emotional understanding of eons. Let's attempt to remedy this in two ways. First, if the height of a six-foot (183 cm) man represents all geological time from the inception of life to the present, then written history is less than the thickness of the epidermal layer on the dome of his skull.

There is another way, a second path to a deeper emotional comprehension of the immensity of evolutionary time. An obscure American journalist, Langdon Smith, wrote a poem of 108 lines titled "Evolution." Martin Gardner, in his book *Order and Surprise*, has written the only existing account of Smith and his one poem. What follows is a quotation from Gardner and the poem's first stanza and final four lines:

> The poem conveys what Darwin had in mind when he wrote, at the close of his *Origin of Species*, "There is grandeur in this view of life." The epic surge of evolution,

from its humble beginning in the dark sea to the mellow light of Delmonico's [restaurant], is caught in this poem as it has not been caught in any other poem before or since:

When you were a tadpole and I was a fish,
In the Paleozoic time,

And side by side on the ebbing tide
We sprawled through the ooze and slime,
Or skittered with many a caudal flip
Through the depths of the Cambrian fen,
My heart was rife with the joy of life,
For I loved you even then.
. . . .
Then as we linger at luncheon here,
O'er many a dainty dish,
Let us drink anew to the time when you
Were a Tadpole and I was a Fish.

It has been a long, long time getting from there to here, and the road has been anything but straight. No life form evolves in a predetermined fashion or direction. It's wondrous, absolutely wondrous, that, as a species, we have continued to exist at all when 99 percent of all others have gone extinct. We didn't descend from angels; rather we ascended from primordial ooze.

The first chapter began with a quotation from T. S. Eliot:

> *We shall not cease from exploration, and the end*
> *of all our exploring will be to arrive where we*
> *started and know the place for the first time.*

The life in, on, and over this land is so gloriously rich, I will never comprehend it all. Here and there, I have gleaned a few truths. Most of what I learned was as a boy wandering these forests, fields, ponds, and streams with my cousin—we learned to love the natural world deeply. But like the woodchuck, I do know one certainty through the science of genetics. The wolf, weasel, whale, and weevil are all related. It is a staggeringly great truth that everything that has ever existed—past or present, living or extinct—is constructed from the same four building blocks—the steps on the DNA molecule.

My Cousin & Me: Lorne & Gordon

This is the only photograph in existence of my cousin and me as boys, and I treasure it. My mother, the person with a camera, took it. Judging by my clothes and the frown on my face, she has dressed me up for this "photo shoot." My cousin in his rubber boots, britches, braces, and shirt is smiling at me ironically thinking, "I'm glad I'm not wearing that."

Also featured in this chapter is a montage of some of the animals we have met in the pages of this book. Long may they burrow, run, and fly through these forests and fields. My cousin and I knew and loved them all.

Here, as Darwin writes, are "forms most beautiful
and most wonderful."

Early in the morning just at sunrise, I leave my home and turn toward the east to watch our star ascend. On the far horizon, I can see a myriad of black specks dancing in the light. At first, I think they are a flock of migrating geese. The rising heat causes the small dark dots to shimmer in the sunlight and wobble from side to side. Occasionally they dip below the horizon and disappear from view. I wait. But they resurface and grow larger. The fluctuations continue with maddening frequency for what seems an eternity, but every time the small black dots reemerge ever larger and closer. I wait! My anticipation increases with the size of the dots. They shimmer, wobble, dip, and resurface like immortals. Again, I wait! Ultimately, I discern some shape. One appears to be a wild stallion with an ape-like being clinging to its back, and the other dots have the vague silhouettes of animals. As they approach, the shapes morph more than the distance should allow. The stallion repeatedly attempts to dislodge the desperate hominid—but the bravery of the rider excites my admiration. I shout encouragement! He doesn't hear me. Again, the rider in the whirlwind appears to transform. Now he rides upright with free hands gripping the reins. Once again, he dips and disappears. And once more, I hold my breath and wait! I cheer as he and all the others miraculously break free of the horizon. Much closer now, he approaches, so that this time he hears me yell. He's so near that I sense his determination and passion for life. The whirlwind of events pummels the rider ever harder; I despair, but he remains mounted with the others at his side. Now I clearly see horse and rider with his companions. He shouts words of recognition. And I know the rider in the whirlwind is my cousin and his companions are all the animals who have found places in our hearts.

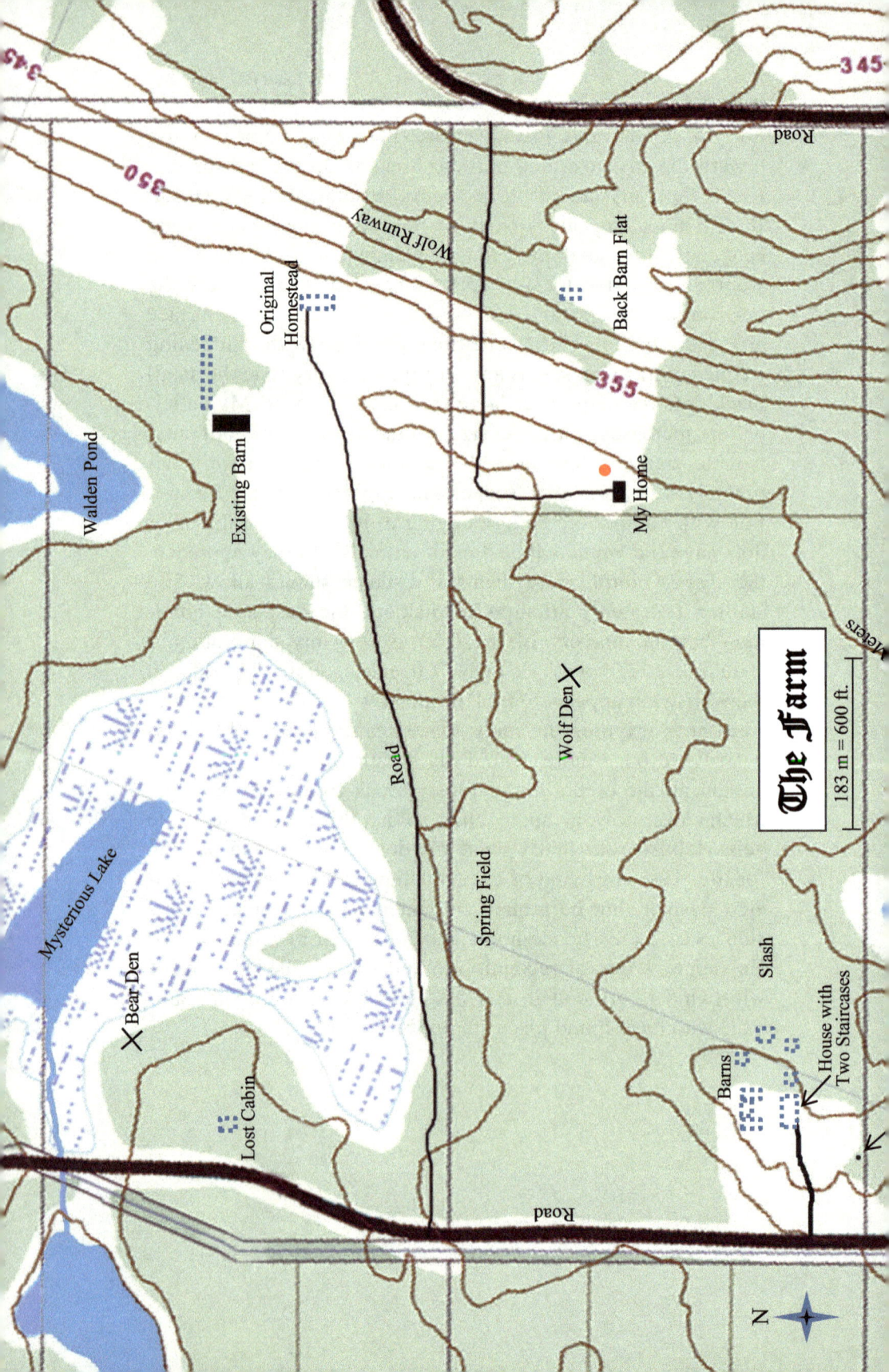

The Farm

183 m = 600 ft.

Meters

Walden Pond

350

345

Existing Barn

Original Homestead

Wolf Runway

355

Back Barn Flat

Road

My Home

Mysterious Lake

Bear Den

Lost Cabin

Road

Wolf Den

Spring Field

Slash

Barns

House with
Two Staircases

Road

N

ENDNOTES

Front Matter
1. Henry David Thoreau, *The Maine Woods*, 7th edition (Boston: James R. Osgood and Company, 1873), 124.

Chapter 1
1. T. S. Eliot, "Little Gidding," in *Four Quartets* (New York: Harcourt, Brace and Co., 1943), 59.
2. Carl Sagan, *Cosmos* (New York: Wing Books, 1995), 233.
3. Charles Darwin, *On the Origin of Species by Means of Natural Selection, Or the Preservation of Favoured Races in the Struggle for Life* (London: John Murray, Albemarle Street, 1861), 525.

Chapter 2
1. Psalm 139:14, Book of Psalms, New International Version.
2. Walt Whitman, *Leaves of Grass* (Philadelphia: David McKay, 1900), line 684.
3. Charles Darwin, *The Expression of the Emotions in Man and Animals* (New York: D. Appleton and Company, 1872), 351.
4. John Keats, "To Autumn," in *The Oxford Book of English Verse, 1250–1900*, ed. Arthur Thomas Quiller-Couch (Oxford, UK: Clarendon, 1919).
5. Omar Khayyám, *The Rubáiyát*, trans. Edward FitzGerald (Boston, MA: Branden Pub. Co., 1989), 40.

Chapter 3
1. Dylan Thomas, "Fern Hill," *Dylan Thomas Selected Poems, 1934–1952* (New York: New Directions, 2003), 170–72.
2. Carl Sagan, quoted in *Textbook of Natural Medicine*, ed. Joseph E. Pizzorno and Michael T. Murray (Edinburgh: Churchill Livingstone, 2012), 143.
3. Heraclitus, "The River-Statement," *A History of Greek Philosophy: Volume 1, The Earlier Presocratics and the Pythagoreans*, ed. William Keith Chambers Guthrie (Cambridge: Cambridge University Press, 1962), 488.

Chapter 4
1. University of Melbourne, "Developing a Global Antidote for Snake Bites: 100,000 People Die from Snake Bites Each

Year," *Science Daily*, December 9, 2008, http://www.sciencedaily.com/releases/2008/11/081127115320.htm.

2. Spielberg, Steven, Douglas Slocombe, George Lucas, Howard Kazanjian, Lawrence Kasdan, Philip Kaufman, Frank Marshall, et al., *Raiders of the Lost Ark* (Hollywood, CA: Paramount, 1981).

Chapter 5

1. John Muir, *John of the Mountains: The Unpublished Journals of John Muir* (Madison: The University of Wisconsin Press, 1979), 82.
2. Friedrich Nietzsche, *Twilight of the Idols*, trans. Duncan Large (Oxford, UK: Oxford University Press, 1998), 5.

Chapter 6

1. Albert Einstein, Letter reprinted in *The New York Times*, March 29, 1972.
2. John Cottingham, "'A Brute to the Brutes?': Descartes' Treatment of Animals," *Philosophy* 53 (1978): 551–59.
3. Voltaire, "Animals," in *The Philosophical Dictionary*, trans. H. I Woolf (New York: A.A. Knopf, 1924), 22.
4. Sociobiologists quotation--- Archana Ruhela, and Malini Sinha, *Recent Trends in Animal Behaviour* (Jaipur, India: Oxford Book Co., 2010), 33.
5. William Blake, "Auguries of Innocence," *The Complete Poetry and Prose of William Blake*, ed. David V. Erdman and Harold Bloom (Berkeley, CA: University of California Press, 2008), 490.
6. Gallup, "Evolution, Creationism, Intelligent Design [May 2014 poll]," *Religion and Social Trends*, http://www.gallup.com/poll/21814/evolution-creationism-intelligent-design.aspx.
7. Dylan Thomas, "Do Not Go Gentle into That Good Night," *Dylan Thomas Selected Poems, 1934–1952* (New York: New Directions, 2003), 122.

Chapter 7

1. Bernd Heinrich, *Bumblebee Economics* (Cambridge, MA: Harvard University Press, 2004), 148–49.
2. Theodosius Dobzhansky, "Nothing in Biology Makes Sense Except in the Light of Evolution," *American Biology Teacher* 35 (1973): 125–29.
3. Jacob Bronowski, *The Ascent of Man* (London: Random House, 2011), 19.

4. "Scientists Solve the 320-Year-Old Mystery of of How the Falklands Wolf Ended up on the Island," *Daily Mail*, March 6, 2013, http://www.dailymail.co.uk/sciencetech/article-2289168/Scientists-solve-320-year-old-mystery-Falklands-wolf-managed-cross-sea-Argentina--say-skated-frozen-sea.html.

5. Charles Darwin, *The Beagle Record: Selections from the Original Pictorial Records and Written Accounts of the Voyage of H.M.S. Beagle*, ed. Richard Darwin Keynes (Cambridge: Cambridge University Press, 2011), 299.

Chapter 8

1. William Blake, "The Tiger," *The Oxford Book of English Verse*, ed. Arthur Quiller-Couch (Oxford: Clarendon, 1919).

2. "Where does" quoted in David Quammen, *The Reluctant Mr. Darwin* (New York: Norton, 2008), 94.

3. W. B. Yeats, "The Lake Isle of Innisfree," in *The Poems of W. B. Yeats: A Routledge Study Guide and Sourcebook*, ed. Michael O'Neill (New York: Routledge, 2003), 97–98.

4. Bernd Heinrich, *The Trees in My Forest* (New York: HarperCollins, 1997), 161.

Chapter 9

1. Lewis Carroll, "The Walrus and the Carpenter," in *Alice's Adventures in Wonderland* (1865; repr., London, UK: Random House, 2012), 230.

2. Stephen Jay Gould, "A Biological Homage to Mickey Mouse," *Ecotone* 4, no. 1 (2008): 333–40.

Chapter 10

1. Alfred, Lord Tennyson, "The Brook," in *Tennyson's Complete Works* (New York: R. Worthington, 1876), 105.

2. Grey Owl, *Pilgrims of the Wild*, ed. Michael Gnarowski (1934; repr., Toronto: Dundurn Press, 2010), 52–53.

3. Robert Bateman, "Hooded Mergansers in Winter," *Robert Bateman: Art Country Canada*, http://www.artcountrycanada.com/bateman-robert-hooded-mergansers.htm.

4. Percy Bysshe Shelley, "The Cloud," in *Ode to the West Wind and Other Poems* (Mineola, NY: Dover Publications, 1993), 57.

Chapter 11

1. Daniel C. Dennett, *Darwin's Dangerous Idea: Evolution and the Meaning of Life* (New York: Simon & Schuster, 1995), 21.

2. Percy Bysshe Shelley, "Ode to the West Wind," in *The Poetical Works of Coleridge, Shelley, and Keats* (Philadelphia: J. Howe, 1831), 209.

Chapter 12
1. Charles Darwin, quoted in *Charles Darwin: Voyaging*, by E. Janet Browne (New York: Knopf Doubleday, 1995), 525.

Chapter 13
1. Dylan Thomas, "The Force that through the Green Fuse Drives the Flower," *The Nation's Favourite: Twentieth Century Poems*, ed. Griff Rhys Jones (London: BBC Books, 1999), 171.
2. Robert Frost, "A Drumlin Woodchuck," in *The Poetry of Robert Frost*, ed. Edward Connery Lathem (New York: Holt Rinehart & Winston, 1967), 281–82.
3. Thornton Wilder, *The Woman of Andros* (London: Longmans, Green, 1954), 20.
4. W. B. Yeats, "The Song of Wandering Aengus," in *The Collected Works of W. B. Yeats, Volume 1: The Poems*, revised 2nd edition, ed. Richard J. Finneran (New York: Simon & Schuster, 2010), 59.

Chapter 14
1. From "What a Wonderful World" by George David Weiss and Bob Thiele, copyright 1967 (Renewed) Quartet Music, Inc. & Range Road Music. All rights reserved. Used by permission.
2. 100 million years --- Dave Goulson, *Bumblebees: Their Behaviour and Ecology* (Oxford: Oxford University Press, 2003), 95.
3. Charles Darwin, Letter to Asa Gray, 22 May [1860], *Darwin Correspondence Project*, https://www.darwinproject.ac.uk/letter/entry-2814.
4. Augustus De Morgan, *A Budget of Paradoxes* (London: Longmans, Green, and Co., 1872), 377.

Chapter 15
1. Jacob Bronowski, *Science and Human Values* (New York: Harper & Row, 1972), 28.
2. Stephen Jay Gould, *Wonderful Life: The Burgess Shale and the Nature of History* (New York: W. W. Norton & Company, 1989), 320.

Chapter 16
1. Fastest flyer "The fastest flying bird in the world is the peregrine falcon. One was recorded flying at 145 kilometers an

hour; but some claim it can fly as fast as 320 kilometers an hour" Sarah Whittley, *All about Birds* (London: New Holland, 2008), 10.

2.   Mark Twain, *The Adventures of Tom Sawyer & The Adventures Huckleberry Finn*, ed. Stuart Hutchinson (Ware, UK: Wordsworth Classics, 1992), 236.

3.   Charles Darwin, *The Descent of Man*, 2 vols. (London: John Murry, 1871), 1:105.

Chapter 17

1.   Jacob Grimm and Wilhelm Grimm, "Little Red-Cap" in *The Fairy Tales of the Brothers Grimm* (Belgrade: Dragan Nikolic, 2012), 51.

2.   Mark Twain, "His Grandfather's Old Ram: Told on the World Tour, 1895–96," *Mark Twain Speaking*, ed. Paul Fatout (Iowa City: University of Iowa Press, 2006), 291.

3.   PBS, "River of No Return: Gray Wolf Fact Sheet," *Nature*, April 13, 2012, http://www.pbs.org/wnet/nature/river-of-no-return-gray-wolf-fact-sheet/7659/

Chapter 18

1.   Jacob Bronowski, *The Ascent of Man* (New York: Random House, 2011), 19.

2.   Al Purdy, "The Country North of Belleville," in *A New Anthology of Canadian Literature in English*, 2nd edition, ed. Donna Bennett and Russell Brown (Toronto: Oxford University Press, 2002), 548–49.

CPSIA information can be obtained
at www.ICGtesting.com
Printed in the USA
BVHW092058180220
572692BV00006B/226